W9-ANZ-765

CAVE TO RENAISSANCE

DRAWINGS OF THE MASTERS

CAVE TO RENAISSANCE

Text by Benjamin Rowland, Jr.
Gleason Professor of Fine Arts
Harvard University

LITTLE, BROWN AND COMPANY · BOSTON · TORONTO

COPYRIGHT © 1965 BY SHOREWOOD PUBLISHERS, INC.

ALL RIGHTS RESERVED. NO PART OF THIS BOOK MAY BE REPRODUCED IN ANY FORM OR BY ANY ELECTRONIC OR MECHANICAL MEANS INCLUDING INFORMATION STORAGE AND RETRIEVAL SYSTEMS WITHOUT PERMISSION IN WRITING FROM THE PUBLISHER, EXCEPT BY A REVIEWER WHO MAY QUOTE BRIEF PASSAGES IN A REVIEW.

A

LIBRARY OF CONGRESS CATALOGING IN PUBLICATION DATA

Rowland, Benjamin, 1904–1972.
Cave to Renaissance.

Reprint of the ed. published by Shorewood Publishers, New York, in series: Drawings of the masters.
Bibliography: p.
1. Drawings. I. Title. II. Series: Drawings of the masters.
NC52.R68 1976 741.9 75-25617
ISBN 0-316-75462-5

Published simultaneously in Canada
by Little, Brown & Company (*Canada*) *Limited*

PRINTED IN THE UNITED STATES OF AMERICA

Contents

CAVE TO RENAISSANCE

"Drawing is the Art of representing the Appearance of Objects, by Imitation; or expressing, by Lines and Shades, the Form or Appearance of any Thing in Nature or Art; the Copying of another Draught, or any Design conceived in the Mind; and all this without the assistance of mathematical Rules."[1†] This quotation from an eighteenth-century manual is as succinct a description of the art of drawing as we could find. This definition would have to be subdivided into a number of modes of expression in draughtsmanship. The first of these would be line drawing, or delineation, in which the whole form is connoted by line alone without regard to local tones or values. This is the most easily legible type of drawing; the subject is marked only by its edges, and the silhouette alone gives an illusion of form. Delineation illustrates the first self-imposed convention of drawing since it begins with line—and there are no lines in nature. The second type of drawing may be called form drawing: this is a mode in which, by shading, the illumination of the surface of an object is conveyed in a limited number of values ranging from light to dark. The drawing is intended to convey a sculpturesque effect, and presumably a sketch of a piece of sculpture would be the most telling example. A final mode has been defined as color-value drawing, in which black-and-white values are intended to approximate the color of objects as well as their form. Engraved copies of paintings would perhaps provide the best example of this attempt to approximate total visual effect in monochrome.

Drawing is a language by which an artist communicates the essentials of some facet of the visual world. Depending on the time and conditions when he works, the artist will relate either what he sees or what he knows about the subject he presents. Also, depending on the climate of the time, he will be

†All footnotes appear on page 52.

drawing either for communication or effect. It is obvious that for primitive artists drawing was a kind of writing. First ideas in drawing are expressed by delineation, and drawing in certain periods never progresses beyond the telling outline. In all traditional art dedicated to the expression of the ultra-real in real terms, the essential symbolical magical elements, rather than naturalism, are uppermost in the artist's mind as is directness in the interest of communication. An aesthetic concern with the technique itself and its manipulation for effect belongs to a different and later phase of development.

Drawing is the basic scaffolding of all artistic expression. It is, to paraphrase a canon of Chinese art, "the bones" of the picture on which everything is hung.[2] Drawing is an adventure, a creative experience in transferring from the mind the imagined shape. Drawing is seeing with the mind as well as the eye.

Drawing in primitive societies may be of magic intent, to make come true what the artist represents as a *fait accompli*. Facts, rather than approximation of total reality, are the aim of such primitive drawing; in other words, the artist presents from memory and experience known realities without mystery or confusion. Drawing in this context is truly a language. The study and recording of actual appearance belong to a later development.

Certain technical devices are specific to drawing. One is, of course, the closed contour which isolates the form on the surface and may suggest either a flat shape or a plastic volume. The open contour is one in which the delineation is broken, so as to suggest a relation between the form and the ambient space denoted by the surface on which it is recorded. In such a drawing the breaking off of strokes may serve to indicate the relative position, forward or back, of the parts of the figure. Specific to draughtsmanship, too, are the effects of form or even color through the thinning and thickening of lines, the placing of heavy accents, or, in form drawing, the shading and hatched strokes or soft, graduated modelling. All of these devices, although they may suggest the effects of painting or sculpture, are aesthetic and technical properties that belong to the art of drawing alone. The delight we find in drawing may derive from the sheer clarity and precision of the consistent organization in line or from the expressive freshness of a spontaneous sketch. In every period of the world's art the drawing, perhaps because of all forms of expression it springs most directly from the artist's reaction to inner vision, is as representative of the climate of a moment in history as the most monumental painting or sculpture.

The early literary references to drawing in the postclassical period consist only of practical suggestions and definitions of traditional procedure. The appreciation of drawings as works of art is a relatively modern, post-Renaissance development, a self-conscious connoisseurship that includes the esteem for sketches as affording the most intimate insight into the artist's personality and emotion. The drawing is, of course, the most telling revelation of the artist's creative process in action. It represents his first conception of a project. In drawing the craftsman is transferring his mental image to paper or parchment. He improvises as the thought develops, and he is at perfect liberty to make alterations and improvements as he realizes his idea through pen or brush. Some drawings, of course, served a purely utilitarian function as guides for a finished composition. Many of these sketches, like the magnificent *sinopie,* or underdrawings, revealed by the restoration of the Campo Santo frescoes, were lost under the painting.[3] We may assume that in some periods the artist was able to work so surely from memory, or to visualize his intended results so clearly, that he dispensed with preliminary sketches and drew directly on panel or wall. For this reason, and because of the perishable nature of drawings, few of them survive from early periods. There is the added fact that, as literary sources inform us, both in antiquity and the Middle Ages artists made their notations on wax tablets which, of course, were not destined to survive.

The autonomous drawing as an end in itself or as a finished product is a rarity in ancient times. The Egyptian sketches, or *ostraka,* are an exception, and it might also be possible to consider the compositions of Greek vases as carefully finished drawings. Such drawings as survive from mediaeval times are either copies of earlier works collected in model books for workshop use or finished drawings intended to serve as patterns for monumental compositions. Only occasionally, in black-and-white illustrations for manuscripts, do we find drawings considered as substitutes for paintings. The casual sketches in margins of codices are among the few examples of autonomous works before the Renaissance period.

The present study will begin with the most primitive known drawing of prehistoric man. As in many later periods, it is sometimes impossible to separate drawing from painting and, in the case of the cavemen, from sculpture or engraving on stone. Our examples of drawing from Egyptian and Mesopotamian antiquity must occasionally depend on paintings and even reliefs to illustrate the development. In the Greek period, the surviving designs of the vase painters belong to the realm of true drawing, but for the Hellenistic and Roman periods we must also analyze the drawing as it appears on painted marble panels. In the mediaeval period we have, of course, many examples of true drawing with pen or brush, but we must on occasion refer to illuminated manuscripts in gouache or watercolor which may be analyzed for their specifically calligraphic characteristics.

THE PREHISTORIC PERIOD

For countless centuries in the Ice Age, the European continent lay infinitely silent under the weight of the great glaciers. The glistening mantle of ice spread over France, Germany, and Scandinavia, and an air view of this frozen world would have looked not unlike the landscape of the polar regions today. In the period when the glaciers began to recede to the valleys of the Pyrenees and the Alps, man's first art appeared. This first dawn of pictorial expression, between 40,000 and 5000 B.C., was the art of the hunters who depended for food and clothing on the great herds of beasts that roamed Europe in this post-glacial age. This is an art magical, rather than aesthetic, in purpose, intended to give the tribe power over, and possession of, the animals drawn by artists dedicated to this cult of hunting magic. The art of the men of the Paleolithic period is located in the depths of grottoes that were used not so much for habitation as for the ritual insuring the success of the hunt. These drawings were not made for public exhibition, nor for the playful joy of the artist in recording aspects of his world. Their very preservation is due to the fact that they were painted deep in natural caves, far from the open air, and their purpose was strictly an utilitarian magical one, a matter of life and death. The effectiveness of the ritual probably depended upon the naturalism of the drawing as a veritable counterfeit of the animal to be conquered. The painted darts and spears are like the pins the witch sticks in the wax effigy of an intended victim in an entirely similar exercise of sympathetic magic. Once the ceremony of "killing" the game in the painted effigy was over and the hunters sallied forth in quest of the real quarry, the drawing lost all further effectiveness, as is indicated by the fact that in many instances at Altamira and Lascaux later drawings and engravings are superimposed on previous efforts.[4]

Since the discovery of the first cave paintings nearly a century ago, scholars have worked out a tentative chronology for these masterpieces of prehistoric art in Spain and France, a cycle that reaches its full maturity in the caves of Lascaux. Primitive man, like the untaught child, expresses himself first in contour delineation that convincingly isolates a single impression from the confusion of reality. And so it is not surprising that the very earliest Aurignacian efforts are entirely in outline or engraving. Only later did sophisticated methods of shading and polychromy seek to improve on these unforgettable and telling silhouettes.

The tools of the prehistoric draughtsmen were a flint burin for engraving and a brush, made perhaps of tufts of hair, feathers, or fur attached to sticks. Reeds or chewed twigs may have been used too, and on occasion colors may have been blown on the wall through a tube. The colors were prepared with charcoal and readily available minerals such as ochre, red chalk, and manganese ore. Chips of red ochre have been found that may have been used like pastel crayons. Generally the colors were applied between the outlines of the drawing and were mixed into a paste with egg white or resin as a binding medium. In some drawings the color was applied directly: the pigment was smeared on, probably with the hand, as a thick paste to fill the contours. Often rather subtle *sfumato* effects of modelling were achieved by the graduated shading rubbed into the local tone.

The draughtsmen who worked in the caves of Altamira, Lascaux, and Les Trois Frères[5] were the greatest animaliers of recorded time. Their beasts have at once a universal and immediate quality. The tremendous bison of Altamira have something of that embodiment of mystical strength, even in death, of Picasso's immortalizations of the bull and the minotaur. The primitive artist, by his emphasis on formidable bulk, seemed always to stress the dangerous power of the hunter's adversary. This is an art that has no equal for characterization of the essentials and life of particular beasts: the mountainous form of the mammoth and elephant, the soft grace of the deer, the tremendous strength of the bison, and the swiftness of the horse. These are memory images and as such they present only what is important to say about an object, visualized in the artist's mind as a clarified image devoid of everything unessential. In their effective presentation of the essential qualities of beast forms, these prehistoric drawings can only be compared with some of the great examples of animal art in India, notably the portrayals of such creatures as the bull and elephant on seals of the Indus Valley period.[6]

Insofar as a chronology for Paleolithic drawings can be established, the earliest Aurignacian type, represented by examples at Altamira and Castillo,[7] is pure line drawing, in which the silhouette of the animal is traced in yellow or red, usually with only the limbs on one side shown. These drawings are simple and ideographic, as correct shorthand presentations of the species as could be imagined. The technique is either engraving or delineation with a primitive brush. This method is followed by one in which color, usually a solid red, is smeared in between the contours. Interior drawing is added, and all limbs are shown. The method is essentially a conceptual one in which, although the animal is shown in profile, the horns of the bison are twisted into a front view. A similar distortion prevails in the drawing of the cloven hooves. In this more plastic vision of the Magdalenian renaissance, the draughtsmen, as at Altamira, would often take advantage of natural bosses on the wall or ceiling of the cave that suggest the general shape of the animal. Drawing around such a protuberance imparts a relief-like effect to what really amounts to a combination of sculpture and draughtsmanship. Hatching or dots, instead of pure outline, occasionally appears. But the draughtsmen of the Ice Age on occasion achieved an extraordinary sophistication in suggesting form in pure line drawing through the use of thick or thin strokes achieved by varying pressure on the brush.

It has been suggested that the Paleolithic artists often worked from sketch sheets, in this case careful engravings on small stone panels, of representations of the beasts which were then enlarged on the walls of the caves. These were the *exempla,* or models, of the prehistoric period, and their existence disproves any theory that the cave drawings were invariably done on the spur of the moment.

The technical development in drawings of the Paleolithic period begins with line drawings in red or yellow, in which the beast forms are presented only in outline silhouettes. Many Aurignacian drawings are really incised

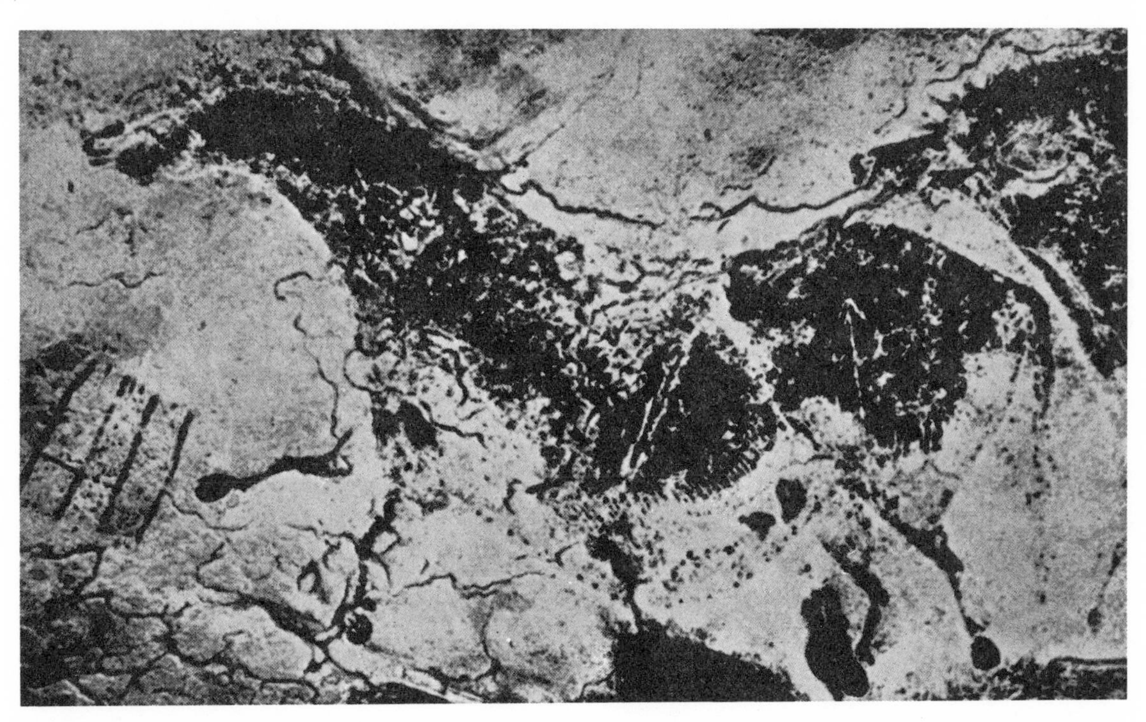

Figure 1

Horse, Magdalenian period • cave painting, height 43¼ inches • Lascaux Cave, France

engravings on the face of the rock; sometimes, but not always, the drawn or incised contours were the bounding outlines for areas of flat tone. Among the more striking examples of the engraved technique are the family of owls in the cavern of Les Trois Frères. These ideographs of birds convey, in their moving simplicity, something of the eternal mystery of the bird of night that we admire today in the paintings of Morris Graves. Some of these earliest Aurignacian drawings, such as the painting of a hairy mammoth at Font-de-Gaume, appear to search for a kind of illusionism in representing the mammal's hairy coat by repeated slanting strokes, rather than solid outline.[8] In the masterpieces of the Magdalenian period, as represented notably by the paintings of Altamira and Lascaux, drawing loses something of its original importance and is replaced by more properly painterly effects of polychromy and suggestions of modelling. The outline, engraved or painted, exists largely to emphasize the new effects of form and color. Although an enhanced naturalism is the rule in the final examples of Magdalenian painting, there is undoubtedly an intrusion of decorative convention that may very possibly reflect the increasing use of prepared sketches intended for enlargement on the cave wall.

EGYPT AND MESOPOTAMIA

When Plato remarked that the art of Egypt remained unchanged for 20,000 years, he was only exaggerating the frozen conventionalism that seems, to the casual observer of today as of the fourth century B.C., to have frozen Egyptian

Figure 2

Egyptian • *Rameses IV in Chariot*, *ca.* 1167–1161 B.C. • painting on stone chip
12 11/16 x 16 5/16 inches • Egyptian Museum, Cairo

art through all the millenia of its development. Suffice it to say that this rigidity and the conceptual, rather than naturalistic, presentation were necessitated by the needs of the state and the state religion. Official art in Egypt was dedicated exclusively to the glorification of the sovereign in a manner that should proclaim in hieratic fashion his grandeur and immortality. Egyptian painting and sculpture were dedicated also to representing in the tomb the persons and objects of everyday life magically necessary for the sustenance of the soul in the long night of immortality. Wall paintings, as much as wall reliefs, were the basic form of expression of this imperial and funerary art. It should be noted that of necessity one of the aims of this art was the recognizable representation of objects within a prescribed conceptual formula. The invariable technique of Egyptian wall paintings involved a preliminary sketch in red, which was subsequently corrected and strengthened with a black brush.

The writing and drawing implement of the Egyptian artist was a rush cut into a chisel shape, so that the sharp edge could be used for fine strokes and a heavier line obtained by using the full width of the implement. This type of pen was only replaced in the Graeco-Roman period by a different type of reed cut like a quill. For painting, brushes made from the fibers of the date palm, of split palm leaves, or of grasses, were generally employed. These coarse, bristle-like points were attached to wooden handles. The black ink used for drawing was manufactured from carbon soot mixed with gum arabic and water.

Throughout its history Egyptian art was devoted to the unquestioned security of convention and the authority of antiquity. This reliance on unvarying law and order governing all experience was as true of the social structure as it was of art. The assurance in fixed canons that developed at a very early period, as a means of imposing both order and immortality on the disturbing variety and disorder of the visual world, in a way militates against the presentation of the real and the immediate. Egyptian art was always one of ideas rather than experience, and the artist was conditioned to draw what he knew rather than what he saw. Such devices as hieratic scaling were parts of a system of representation in which such *a priori* conventions replaced the portrayal of things as they are.

The conventions of Egyptian drawing developed from the same conceptual logic as the hieroglyphs, which are, of course, readable pictures. Ultimately this ordered rendering of the essentials of forms stems from the conceptual viewpoint of the prehistoric period. The dependence on outline drawing might be regarded as another and more sophisticated continuation of the tradition of Paleolithic drawing. The entirely conceptual ideation of the human figure goes back to the beginnings of Egyptian drawing. It is invariably a composite memory picture of the body from the most characteristic points of view, with the face in profile, the eye in full face, the torso in front view, and the legs in side view. The proportions were fixed by a strict geometric canon, in which the true nature of existence was to be expressed by numbers, and the measurement of the figure to be determined by the proportionate width and length of the fingers, arms, and other members in relation to the whole. This is an approach that led to the creation of a world of forms apart from—and superior to—nature. Only on rare occasions did Egyptian art depart from this kind of schematization that was entirely independent of the real appearance of objects in the visual world. One of these moments came in the Eighteenth Dynasty during the reign of Ikhnaton, or Amenhotep IV. This ruler, it will be remembered, established the monotheistic worship of the sun-god Aten, with an emphasis on truth. Since it followed that everything natural must always be true, this concept led to a temporary end of the old formality in art. The drawings from this period are marked by refinement and elegance and a strangely expressionistic realism. There is a new freedom in the drawing of human figures marked by attempts to represent them in three-quarter and frontal view.

Egyptian drawings survive principally in the form of the so-called *ostraka,* limestone chips used as sketch pads by artists as a substitute for the expensive papyrus. Sometimes the drawings are sketches for compositions in relief or painting, for example the subjects from the reign of Rameses III. These preliminary drawings are designed in accordance with the usual conventions and proportions of monumental art, but are executed in a rapid and sure freehand manner as memory images of familiar themes. Much more expressive are the animal caricatures, satires on the pomp and circumstance of a decadent and sophisticated society. Some, like the cat and mouse enacting the roles of servant and mistress, drawn with powerful rough strokes, evoke the spirit of the great animal caricatures of Toba Sojo, the famous animalier of the Fujiwara period in Japan.[9] The same subjects occasionally appear in more refined papyrus scrolls. Other papyri provide illustrations of the Egyptian *exempla,* models for standard subjects drawn in a hard, diagrammatic fashion and squared with grids to determine the fixed proportions and to allow for enlargement. One of the finest surviving Egyptian drawings is the preparatory outline for a wall painting that was never completed: this is the portrait of Senmut,

Queen Hatshepsut's favorite, at Deir-el-Bari, a drawing that not only reveals the amazing sureness with which the artist drew in even, unbroken lines, but also shows us how a moving characterization of a real person could be achieved within the rigid conceptual formula for the human head.

Examples of drawing and painting from the period of the great monarchies of the ancient Near East are so rare that it is impossible to present any kind of historical development of this technique. It is only possible to suggest that drawing must have followed the canons and stylistic character of Mesopotamian relief sculpture.

One of the relics of pure drawing, or engraving on metal, from Mesopotamian antiquity is the silver vase of King Entemena of Lagash. This beautiful object, found at Telloh, dates from the third millennium B.C. A design, including fantastic winged beasts, is incised on the surface of the metal. The engraving displays a real draughtsmanly quality, not only in the refined, wiry precision but in the subtle variations in the thickness of lines to suggest form on the flat surface.

Among the few examples of Mesopotamian painting are the fragments of a wall painting of an investiture scene in the Palace of Mari, which may date from the time of the great Hammurabi. The outlines of the forms were literally engraved on the wet plaster with a stylus-like implement. If the stiff and lifeless drawing of the human figures seems like an enlargement of a cylinder seal, with the decadence of an earlier tradition, the drawing of such details as the palm tree filled with birds reveals an extraordinary ease and sureness in the rendering, a combination of observation of natural forms and a sense for decoration. Especially notable is the single figure of a bird, in which the fluffy character of the plumage is indicated by the use of hatchings, rather than a closed outline, for the silhouette.

Another site that has yielded a considerable number of Assyrian wall paintings of the eighth century B.C. is Til Barsip on the upper Euphrates. Many of the subjects represented, like the horsemen, are the pictorial counterparts of the favorite themes of Assyrian reliefs. The conceptual representation of these and other figures will of course recall the conventions of Egyptian art. The drawing of the outlines in thick, heavy lines serves to emphasize the schematic and essentially decorative concept of the form. Both the figures and the method of execution have something of the overpowering heaviness and static quality of Assyrian sculpture. As in the famous hunting reliefs from Nineveh, the most memorable aspect of the Til Barsip paintings is in the telling recording of small details. These few fragments of Assyrian drawing and painting represent a dead end rather than a beginning. Like the more famous sculptures, they were dedicated entirely to the glorification of the monarchy. This was an art not for export, but for enriching the life of the palace, which, with the destruction of the Assyrian Empire, came to an end.

GREECE AND ROME

Our knowledge of the beginnings of drawing in ancient Greece is complicated by the fact that the same words are used to describe both drawing and painting in Greek and Latin. This is perhaps to be taken as an indication of the importance attached to outline. Pliny, one of our great sources for the history of ancient arts, asserts that the first step in the development of figure drawing consisted in tracing the shadow of a man with lines. He uses the term *"monochromatum"* to describe the earliest types of painting, which were apparently outlines filled with a single color.[10]

Pliny sums up the esteem in which the connoisseur of antiquity held outline delineation when he says, in discussing the famous master Parrhasios:

> He is unrivalled in the rendering of outline. This is the highest subtlety attainable in painting. Merely to paint a figure in relief is no doubt a great achievement... but where an artist is rarely successful is in finding an outline which shall express the contours of the figure. For the contour should appear to fold back, and so enclose the object as to give assurance of the parts behind, thus clearly suggesting even what it conceals. (*Nat. Hist.,* XXXV, 67–68)

There could be no more succinct definition of line drawing communicating the idea of form and substance. Further betokening this Roman admiration for draughtsmanship is Pliny's remark: "Many other traces of his draughtsmanship remain, both in pictures [*tabulae*] and on parchments which are said to be instructive to artists." (*Nat. Hist.,* XXXV, 68)

Before Pliny, Dionysos of Halikarnassus had written:

> In ancient painting the scheme of coloring was simple and presented no variety in the tones; but the line was rendered with exquisite perfection, thus lending to these early works a singular grace. This purity of draughtsmanship was gradually lost; its place was taken by a learned technique, by the differentiation of light and shade, by the full resources of the rich coloring, etc. (*de Isaco iudic.* 4)

Other authorities, such as Vitruvius, speak of the existence of drawings for architectural projects and maps. Pliny, as noted, mentions how artists of later periods learned from the sketches on parchment by Parrhasios. This is in itself highly suggestive of the method, followed throughout the Middle Ages, of learning from copies of earlier works.

The implements for drawing in ancient Greece and Rome were the stylus and a fine brush described as a *penicillus*. Brushes made of bristles and soft sponges were also in use, and pencils and crayons of red ochre and charcoal were also employed. For fine drawings on papyrus or parchment, a reed pen came into use as early as the third century B.C.

Classical literature, both Greek and Latin, is filled with references to famous Greek painters, such as Polygnotus, Parrhasios, Apelles, and Zeuxis,[11] but not a single work by these artists has survived. On the other hand, the signed works of scores of vase painters from the sixth to the fourth century are known. But not one of these men is alluded to by Pliny or Pausanias. Vase painting was regarded as a craft, rather than a major art, its products dedicated to the temple and private use. We can be sure in many cases that the

Figure 3

Apollo, Leto, Artemis, 650–600 B.C.
painting on Melian *amphora*
National Archaeological
Museum, Athens

Figure 4

DOURIS • *Eos and Memnon*, 490–480 B.C.
red-figured *kylix* • diameter of *kylix* 10½ inches
Louvre, Paris

compositions and the figure drawing of the vase paintings reflect the performance of the great mural and easel painters of the time, and that the essentials of draughtsmanship were the same for both. The designs of both black-figure and red-figure vases were perforce simplifications of monumental painting, but the decoration of the so-called white-ground *lekythoi* suggests the paintings on white wood panels and parchment mentioned by classical writers.

It would be impossible in the present work to give a detailed chronological history of the vastly complicated development of draughtsmanship on Greek vases from the seventh to the fourth century. It will suffice to present a few telling examples of the principal moments in this chronology. Painting and drawing began in Greece after the collapse of the earlier Mycenaean civilization, *ca.* 1000 B.C. These beginnings are already marked by a strong originality quite different from the earlier Oriental traditions. The earliest phase of Greek drawing may be represented by the so-called Dipylon vases of the ninth century.[12] The drawing consists of an allover pattern of geometric designs arranged in panels and bands, interspersed with schematic representations of human and animal figures. The bodies of the figures are invariably composed of superimposed triangles with sticklike legs, a convention that seems completely in keeping with the geometric character of the ornament. There is a feeling of almost mathematical orderliness. The conventions are handled so consistently and easily that it is necessary to assume the existence of a long tradition to explain this very sophisticated formalized decoration. Other painted wares from Corinth and Rhodes of the eighth and seventh centuries display an Oriental influence in the presentation of stylized, fantastic beasts,

Figure 5

Portrait of an Imperial Family from ms. IB18, 7th century A. D. • pen and ink
Biblioteca Nazionale, Naples

and in a tendency to fill every available space with geometric or foliate ornaments.

The beginnings of true Greek drawing and painting are to be found in certain works of the sixth century, when draughtsmanship began to exist for its own sake and the human figure took its place as the dominant motif. A masterpiece of this period is the so-called François Vase, painted *ca.* 550 B.C. The world of mythology becomes the principal theme, and the François Vase includes many of the subjects from the Achilles and Theseus stories that were to be repeated over and over again. The emphasis is now largely on narrative, and the human figures, although still conceptually rendered, are no longer composed of decorative triangles, as in the geometric period. The figures are finely incised and their outlines filled in with black against the clay ground of the vase. White is used for the flesh of women, and there are occasional touches of purple. The drawing shows a new freedom and delight in the portrayal of action and varied poses. The vase bears the signature of the painter Klitias, thus marking the first recorded appearance of an autonomous draughtsman in the history of Greek art.

Greek art can be said to have begun when artists discovered the human figure as a form useful not only for decorative purposes, but as a thing of beauty in itself. From this moment on, the development moved towards the representation of humans with reference to nature and with a growing awareness of the beauty of their organic articulation and its revelation through action. The decorative always came first in vase painting, and the shape of these vessels to a certain extent conditioned subjects and compositions according to fixed schemes. The schemes of spacing, of course, go back to the geometric patternizing of the Dipylon vases, but, by the middle of the sixth century, we note an infinite variety within these set arrangements, and, what is even more important, a striving for beauty of form within these self-imposed canons.

The so-called black-figure style of vase painting, in which human figures and details of setting appear as dark silhouettes against the red clay of the background, was already announced in the François Vase and makes its appearance as a universal style about 550 B.C. At this period the names of many artists appear on the decorations of vessels of all types.

Perhaps the greatest draughtsman in the black-figure style was the vase painter who signed himself "Exekias." Some of his designs, like the cup with Dionysos sailing in a vine-clad skiff surrounded by dolphins, perpetuate the feelings of the earliest vase painters for the ornamental filling of a space, together with the wonderful suggestion of movement in the precisely etched shapes. "Etched" is a word deliberately chosen to describe the technique of the black-figure painters, because in this example, as in another masterpiece that shows Achilles and Ajax playing draughts, the lines of contour and interior drawing are incised into the black glaze in a manner that amounts to engraving. The bilateral symmetry of the arrangement is typical of this period and so, too, is the rich pattern of the drapery described in finely scratched lines. Running figures with bent legs are sometimes used to fill the circular *kylix* form. In all black-figure drawings, the human forms have a brittle, weightless, and entirely flat quality brought about partly by their conception as black silhouettes, partly by the extremely light, wiry character of the line engraving.

Perhaps the greatest change in the development of Greek drawing came with the change from the black-figure to the red-figure style *ca.* 530 B.C. This method was simply the reverse of the earlier style, with the black glaze applied to the background, leaving the figures and details of setting relieved in the red ground color of the clay. To be sure, in vases of the transitional period the new style is simply a transliteration of the black-figure technique, and the figures are still patternized to a certain extent. But there is a gradual disappearance of the decorative ornateness of the earlier tradition and an emergence of a new freedom and skill in drawing, together with a consummate understanding of anatomy that parallels contemporary developments in Greek sculpture.

The character of the new style can be seen at its best in a number of vase drawings by the painter Euphronius. One of these is the representation of the combat between Herakles and Antaios, which reveals a great advance in the rendering of anatomy thought to be due to the innovations of the artist Kimon, known only from literary sources. The design shows far less flatness than any earlier work, and its power derives largely from the freedom of drawing with the brush that has replaced the earlier incised technique. This is a magnificent illustration of the dependence of Greek painting on draughtsmanship, in which line conveys all that it is necessary to know about form and movement. Although the figures are still somewhat schematically treated, there is a new accuracy and precision in the rendering of anatomical details, such as the abdominal muscles. Perhaps there is an echo of monumental painting in the grand scale of the forms and in the dramatic expression of agony. What strikes us above all are the advances in the suggestion of the mass and foreshortening of the figures through the refined brush drawing.

In the designs of the red-figure vases of the late sixth and early fifth centuries we begin to see reflections of the new naturalism and monumentality in the conception of the human figure that characterized Greek sculpture of this same period. The powerful figures, like the Herakles and Antaios by the painter Euphronios, are drawn with fine lines, schematized but with an obvious reference to organic articulation and with regard to perspective and foreshortening of the forms. The old feeling for the ornamental persists in many drawings, especially in the fanlike archaic drapery of such works as the *Peleus and Thetis* by Peithinos, and even in such a noble design as the *Eos and Memnon* by Douris that is like a prophecy of the Avignon *Pietà*.[13] The development of a truly heroic style may be seen in many vase drawings of the second quarter of the fifth century, such as the famous *Achilles Slaying Penthesilea,* in which the drawing is more fluid and strong, and the element of pathos, perhaps under the influence of the famed wall painter Polygnotus, appears for the first time.

We enter a new chapter in the history of Greek draughtsmanship with the vase painters of the second quarter of the fifth century, whose works show something of the grandeur of monumental art. This painting displays a new largeness of style and yet still retains an appropriate effect of flatness in the continuing emphasis on contour and profile. There is a new suggestion of depth in the overlapping of the forms. The large and still formal drawing of the figures, together with the restraint and dignity, even in violent subjects, is evocative of the heroic grandeur of the Olympia pediments.[14]

A group of vases attributed to an artist known as the Niobid Painter is always cited as a reflection of monumental painting, notably the famous cycle by Polygnotus at Delphi. The key monument of this group is the Niobid Vase representing Apollo and Artemis slaying the children of Niobe. This drawing differs from other compositions we have examined, in that the figures are no longer grouped in a frieze, but are placed on different levels. Classical literary accounts inform us that this arrangement was often to be seen in the lost monumental paintings of classical antiquity.

To this same tradition of monumental figure drawing belong the designs incised on ivory panels discovered in the Crimea. A beautiful engraving of Athena and Aphrodite, dating from the late fifth century, is executed in a fine light line that suggests both the heroic grandeur and dignity of the goddesses, reminiscent of the sculpture of the Parthenon,[15] and beautifully suggests, through loops and broken lines, the articulation of the thin material enclosing their forms. Compared with earlier examples, the drawing has a florid quality in the description of details and a kind of final academic perfection of a classic moment.

A type of Greek drawing that not only approaches our modern idea of draughtsmanship, but also approximates the effects of the lost works of Greek easel and mural painting, is to be seen in the decoration of the funeral vases known as white-ground *lekythoi*. This technique of drawing on a white ground is also known in a number of beautiful designs on *kylix* cups. The preliminary drawing consisted of light lines scratched into the white slip in a manner approximating silverpoint. The white ground itself, of course, gives the effect of paper or parchment, and we are much more conscious of the easy, controlled lines that describe in shorthand the beauty of the bodily forms and drapery.

Many of the drawings on the white-ground *lekythoi* of the later fifth century, like the beautiful example in Athens or the *Woman by a Tomb* in the collection of antiquities at Munich, display a new interest in sketchy freedom of draughtsmanship that suggests the derivation of many of Picasso's drawings in this lyric mode of linear definition.[16] Something of an expression of *ethos* is present in the recording of the mourner's poignant absorption, sunk in sorrow by the tomb. These drawings from the last quarter of the fifth century have the freshness of a charcoal sketch.

We can get some idea of the nature of Greek monumental drawing from a number of marble panels, painted in monochrome, from Herculaneum. One of these, representing a tense game of jackstones or knucklebones, is a counterpart of the Phidian style, with heavy brush lines similar to the draped forms of the *Three Fates* of the Parthenon. Other paintings of this type, associated with the famous Zeuxis, give the impression of the great monumental cartoons of the Renaissance and are beautifully drawn in a combination of contour and finely hatched shading in a reddish monochrome. A marble gravestone shows a monochrome sketch of the warrior Rhynchon, actually the underdrawing of a picture originally finished in encaustic. The slighter, more elegant form reflects the canon of Praxiteles or Lysippus, and the drawing has become more refined and ornate.

Actual drawings of the Graeco-Roman period are extremely rare, but a number of examples, all of them book illustrations, have been found at Oxyrhynchus in Egypt. The finest of these is a fragmentary drawing on papyrus, representing an episode from the legend of Cupid and Psyche and probably dating from no later than the second century A.D. The drawing must have been made with an Egyptian rush stylus. The draughtsmanship reveals an exquisite sensitivity in the tracing of the delicate, hair-thin contours. A sense of form and plasticity is communicated by the interior drawing in a technique that appears to be a refined perpetuation of the technique of the Greek white-ground *lekythoi* of the Great Period. In its suggestions of statuesque monumentality it would not be difficult to imagine this drawing enlarged to the composition of a wall painting.

Another fourth-century fragment, now in the State Library at Munich, depicts Briseis led away by the heralds, an episode from the first book of the *Iliad*. The drawing of this dramatic episode has become quite cursive in quality, and the somewhat clumsy articulation of the figures indicates that we are dealing with a work of the Late Antique period. Here, as so often in the sculpture and monumental painting of the Late Antique period, a kind of expressionistic vigor and crudity replace the refinement of earlier times.

A final example of drawing of the late Roman period may be found in a fragment of a *rotulus,* again from Oxyrhynchus, dealing with the legend of Herakles. Frameless drawings accompanied by text illustrate the hero's adventure with the Nemean lion. The drawings are extremely sketchy and cursive, so that they appear almost like hieroglyphs rather than finished drawings. The rather careless draughtsmanship, together with the reduction of the human figure to a kind of ideograph, forecasts the point of view of the mediaeval period, which witnessed the death of the gods and the exile of the human figure into a world unreal in terms of both form and space.

THE MIDDLE AGES

Scholars are divided on the question of the very existence of what we would call autonomous drawings during the Middle Ages. Some hold that in the mediaeval craft tradition there was no place for independent artistic expression and that drawings were made only for certain definite purposes.[17] Others maintain that we can find occasional examples of drawings made for their own sake in the period before the Renaissance. Certain types of drawing obviously were prepared for utilitarian ends. These would include copies of earlier paintings and sculptures as an aid to memory or for transmitting traditional forms. Also in this category are the drawings in *exempla,* or model books, collections of plans, and drawings of natural objects made by a master for his own use and for his studio. There are, of course, also many examples of preliminary drawings or underdrawings made specifically for manuscript illustrations with pen or lead-point stylus.

For examples of original or autonomous drawings we would have to examine the casual sketches made by scribes in codices and certain drawings for miniatures, made as finished works in monochrome. Nature studies, made from life rather than from memory or models, do not occur until the very end of the mediaeval period, when the attitude towards the real world was approaching the empirical outlook of the Renaissance.

For our purposes the Middle Ages may be thought of as extending from the end of the Western Roman Empire in the fifth century until the beginnings of the Renaissance in the fourteenth.

Not only was the mediaeval artist completely subordinated to the dictates of the church and dedicated to fulfilling its needs, but many other factors that separated mediaeval thought from both the classic and Renaissance outlooks also governed his performance. The copying of nature did not exist, and the apprentice learned by copying models or *exempla,* many of which undoubtedly went back to the antique period. In this endless process of repetition, successive copies became more and more schematic, and the essentials of movement and life came more and more to be portrayed in terms of calligraphy, rather than in form and texture. This reduction of the beauty of natural forms to diagrammatic simplicity was, of course, completely appropriate to that suppression of all sensual beauty that was part of the Christian artist's revolt against the pagan past.

The draughtsman's use of *exempla* was a practice that obviated the necessity of drawing from nature in the same way that systems of proportion—based not on human beauty but on an abstract mathematical ratio, especially as developed in Byzantium—prescribed the drawing of figures which, by virtue of the perfection of their proportions in a canon of numbers of divine import, would be more beautiful than any created on the accidental basis of a human model. The development of dynamic calligraphic drawing under the influence of barbarian design in the Celtic world provided a technique not only beautiful and consistent in itself, but also significant as a means for insuring an abstract supernatural distortion of forms transcending reality. What we think of as the abstraction or disembodiment of forms in mediaeval drawing may stem from the tenets of Neoplatonism: that the artist cannot be satisfied with a mere transcription of physical appearance, but must strive to portray the spiritual nature imprisoned in the physical body. Such an idea could only be

Figure 6

Illustration from *Fables of Avianus*, 9th century A.D. • pen and ink
Bibliothèque Nationale, Paris

Figure 7

Italian • *Madonna* from ms. Reg. lat. 2090
11th–13th century A.D. • pen and ink
Biblioteca Vaticana, Rome

achieved by a conscious return to the ancient Oriental concepts of hieratic formality and by a conceptual, rather than naturalistic, approach.

As late as the thirteenth century, in the model book of Villard de Honnecourt, we encounter a reliance on geometry as a means of achieving the true spiritual nature of things. As this craftsman tells us, "In this book can be found good advice upon the art of drawing as geometry directs and teaches it."[18] Villard coerces the forms of humans, animals, and even statues into interlocking geometric shapes. These material images are constructed according to geometric patterns, diagrams that in their purity and finality eliminate everything accidental, and present what St. Thomas Aquinas meant by the higher spiritual nature of things of this world perfected in the soul.[19] In Villard's book the natural shapes the artist observed in nature are invariably accommodated to mathematical canons, so that, no matter what subject he draws, the artist achieves ornamental regularity in place of the imitation of nature.

Drawing in line seems to have exerted a quite unique enchantment over artists in mediaeval times. Whereas in antiquity, as Pliny suggests, it was the primary function of line, especially in the delineation of contours, to suggest the full existence of the forms bounded, in the Middle Ages the corporeal existence of the figure was no longer of importance, and the line of the artist's pen or brush suggested, if anything, insubstantiality rather than mass. Line, especially in the modes of draughtsmanship derived from the barbarian styles of ornament, became an instrument for endless invention and magical convolutions. The representation of figures was conditioned by the rhythmic flourishes of penmanship that was both an end in itself and a means of suggesting, in appropriately abstract framework, the unreality of beings and events in the invisible other world. Such surviving *exempla* as the Prudentius of Adémar de Chabannes, although going back to Late Antique originals, reveal how little the eleventh-century artist cared for the classic prototype in his new interest in purely linear expression. It is as though this calligraphic schematization, like Villard de Honnecourt's geometric diagrams, were intended to express the inner essential character and spiritual harmony of things in this world. What to the modern eye appears as abstraction or distortion in mediaeval drawing was also affected by the magic of numbers, especilly with regard to canons of proportion. The number three, standing for the Trinity, is at the basis of the Byzantine canon of nine heads for the total height of the figure. These magical numerical ratios are also at the basis of the geometrical forms in which human figures were enclosed.

What we think of as the classical tradition—with its devotion to the concrete definition of form, particularly the human figure, and the illusionistic representation of space and light—did not come to an abrupt end with the fall of the Western Roman Empire in the fifth century. It survived in many forms throughout the history of Byzantine art, notably in specific references to pagan themes and in the treatment of the human figure and its setting. At the same time, under the influence of the same Oriental hieraticism and ornamental formality that affected the ritual of the court of the Eastern Empire, Byzantine drawings, like their counterparts in mosaic and painting, present the human figure as a phantom shape in a world without space, conceived more as surface ornament than plastic form. This abstraction or spiritualization of antique form was entirely appropriate to expressing the mystical ideals of Christianity through the very negation of the physical existence and beauty of corporeal forms.

The classical tradition enjoyed a rebirth, or *renovatio,* in the Carolingian period. The term "renaissance" is applied to this era because of the conscious effort on the part of the Emperor Charlemagne to inaugurate a renewal of the Roman Empire in jurisprudence, politics, learning, and the arts. The fruits of this policy may be seen in many famous manuscripts such as the Schatzkammer Gospels, in which the broad handling of the figures of the Evangelists and the impressionistic treatment of the landscape are a shorthand linear approximation of the ancient illusionistic technique. The result of combining the classic or Late Antique formula of figure drawing with the more dynamic quality of northern or Celtic draughtsmanship may be seen in a number of Carolingian manuscripts associated with the scriptorium of Reims, notably the Gospels of Bishop Ebbo. On the pages of this manuscript, the figures of the Evangelists are drawn with a brush loaded with white, moving in a rapid zigzag pattern. There is an explosive quality about this rapid linear formula. Although the artist must have had an antique model before him, the shapes are really conceived in terms more of calligraphy than plastic form, and the dazzling whiteness of the web of moving lines makes them loom as a strange, disembodied, phosphorescent bonfire of ghostly power rather than as solid shapes.

One of the most remarkable collections of mediaeval drawings is to be found in the pages of the Utrecht Psalter, another example of the explosive type of draughtsmanship seen in the Ebbo Gospels. The illustrations are literal translations of the phrases of the Psalms into pictorial equivalents, all enclosed in vast, embracing landscapes ultimately reminiscent of such Roman works as the *Odyssey* landscapes.[20] Although the interpretation of the Psalms may be based on earlier commentaries, and the style may be based on Late Antique illustrations, the dynamic draughtsmanship transforms the classic model into a completely new idiom. The artist, or scribe, has been literally carried away by the decorative and emotional possibilities of his penmanship. The staccato zigzag strokes of the artist's pen not only effect a complete coherence of all parts of the diverse composition, but also provide an extraordinary sensation of turbulent movement and energy. At the same time these nervous strokes translate the sense of space and light of the old Roman illusionistic technique into dynamically simplified form.

The Utrecht Psalter was apparently imported to England at an early period and was destined to exercise great influence on the development of mediaeval English draughtsmanship. The Harley Psalter is actually a free copy of it, with even more dynamically animated calligraphy. The great school that flourished at Winchester under St. Aethelwold in the eleventh century was an outgrowth of this style. Some of the manuscripts executed there in pen drawing on white parchment display the greatest possible refinement in calligraphic drawing. The fantastic attenuation and dynamic agitation of the human figures anticipate the Burgundian school of Romanesque sculpture.[21]

One of the great masterpieces of draughtsmanship of the Winchester school is a drawing in brownish red ink of the Crucifixion. This drawing, dating from the last decades of the tenth century, is another manifestation of the influence of the wildly nervous draughtsmanship of the Utrecht Psalter and the Ebbo Gospels. The drawing is executed in brownish red outline with flickering touches of black strokes. The forms have the frail insubstantiality and brittleness of autumn leaves. The figures lean in yearning sorrow towards the Crucified, and the very direction of the crackling and moving lines seems calculated, in an expressionistic way, to indicate their passionate grief. The line of the serrated contours is broken at intervals as though to impart a feeling of form to these shapes in an unreal world. Contrasting with the emotionally agitated draughtsmanship of the attendant figures is the calm, relatively unbroken drawing of the figure of Christ, serene in death. As always in the drawings of the Winchester school, we admire the beautiful consistency of the strokes of calligraphic force and the sparkling richness of the darker accents on the surface of the page.

The artistic ancestors of the late mediaeval style in all the arts are the tradition of classical draughtsmanship and the style of the barbarian peoples of northern Europe. Classical art, modified by the intrusion of Oriental influences towards formality and hieraticism, provided the loom for the creations of Byzantine art. The style of barbarian art derives ultimately from the ancient crafts of the various tribes, some of them of Eastern origin, who became the masters of northern Europe and Scandinavia during the so-called Dark Ages. This art—Lombard, Germanic, or Norse—has certain common factors: a fondness for fantastic beast forms, and a reduction of every representational element into elusive and dynamic thickets of convoluted interlace, in which neither plasticity nor biological accuracy are of any importance. The creatures and the designs they fill are in a continuous process of protean change and movement. In drawing, the principal monuments of this passionate invention of the fantastic are the manuscripts illuminated in the remote Irish

Figure 8
Villard de HONNECOURT
Studies of Men and Beasts, from ms. fr. 19093, ca. 1225–50 A.D.
leadpoint reinforced with pen lines on parchment • 9$\frac{1}{16}$ x 5$\frac{15}{16}$ inches
Bibliothèque Nationale, Paris

monasteries of the seventh and eighth centuries. The rise of Ireland as a great cultural center began with the conversion of the island by St. Patrick in 431. The great renaissance of Celtic art lasted from the mid-seventh century until the disastrous Viking invasions that began in 795. There is no remote suggestion of reality in the Irish manuscripts, but rather representations of a changing magical world of enmeshed details, like a maze or labyrinth inviting endless inspection. The figures in Celtic manuscripts are reduced to a language of wirelike lines that suggest precious inlays of enamel and gold. The manuscripts of the Celtic renaissance, in their tortured convolutions of lines, evoke the strange relation between beings and inanimate things and the magical metamorphosis in Irish legends, such as the *Ballad of Tuan MacCairill:*

> A hawk today, a boar yesterday,
> Wonderful instability!
> Dearer to me every day
> God, the friend who chooses my shape.[22]

The draughtsmanship of the Gospels of Armagh and Lichfield is of marvellously precise, wirelike fineness and an inventive intricacy that suggest its origin in the fantastic and completely nonclassical art of the barbarian past.

Just as Greek drawing parallels forms of expression in monumental art, so many fragments of mediaeval draughtsmanship are the equivalents of the styles of painting and sculpture. This is especially notable in a Romanesque drawing from Anchin: the frail, chrysalis-like form of the Trinity and the towering St. George could with little difficulty be translated into the twelfth-century sculpture of Chartres. Villard de Honnecourt's drawings are in many cases the artist's linear transcription of the antique sculptural style of Reims.

Copies in mediaeval times were a means of preserving admired compositions in wall painting or mosaic, and also served as a point of departure for the artist's own creative expression. Such is the thirteenth-century page, with the representation of the Forty Martyrs, that follows known prototypes in a variety of media. The drawing, especially in the generalized monumental figures and the linear convolutions of the drapery, suggests a later period than the original, and may be described as a creative copy. Certain sketches in codices suggest the form world of barbarian ornament, and the fantastic dragon in a Montecassino manuscript might have been inspired by an Oriental aquamanile. Even the three-pointed pen scratches that fill the outline seem like a calligrapher's imitation of metal engraving.

The drawings in a Byzantine model book in the Vatican present sketches of conventional types of the Madonna and one of St. Francis that not only bear a resemblance to examples of Byzantine and Romanesque painting in Italy, but also clearly reveal the standard Byzantine canon for the head, based on a circle and symmetrically balanced on the median line. These prescriptions were so well known to the artist that he has executed them freehand in easy, flowing pen strokes to produce designs so simplified that they have the air more of diagrams than of finished drawings.

The most famous of all the model books is the collection of sketches compiled by Villard de Honnecourt in the thirteenth century. It contains architectural projects, such as the tower of Laon Cathedral; human figures, some from antique and Gothic sculpture; and drawings of various birds and beasts. Like all *exempla,* the book was made for utilitarian purposes, and some of the drawings were strengthened by the artist or by a workshop assistant long after they were first set down. The preliminary drawings were done with a lead-point stylus and then gone over with the pen. Some of Villard's drawings, like the lion, have notations indicating they were done from life.[23] This frontally rigid beast is an illustration of how the mediaeval artist, even if he did see a real lion, mentally transposed nature into his memory of some heraldic animal and into the usual framework of geometric shapes. In Villard's drawings of antique statues and Gothic sculpture,[24] the nude anatomy and the drapery folds are systematized with his formula of repeated hairpin lines. The monumentality and comparative naturalism of his drawings derive from his study of nature and sculpture, but in his final sketches these sources are invariably standardized in accordance with geometric proportions and calligraphic conventions.

One of the most remarkable documents in the history of Western art and science is the famous manuscript of Frederick II's treatise on falconry, *De Arte Venandi cum Avibus.*[25] This thirteenth-century work was one of the first to substitute the testimony of empirical research for the purely legendary and allegorical conception of nature in scholastic philosophy, and it is not surprising that the illustrations for the book should match this approach. The drawings, which describe the habits and appearance of many varieties of birds, show the first attempt to differentiate between species. The draughtsmanship, as illustrated by an underdrawing of two riding falconers, is executed in rapid pen strokes and bears no suggestion of the accommodation to geometric figures in Villard de Honnecourt's model book. Among the related spontaneous sketches are representations of dancers and other secular forms in the margins of a North Italian Bible of the twelfth century. These casual sketches seem to reveal for the first time a delight in linear expression for its own sake and a feeling for a free and artistic organization in rhythmic curves.

Late Gothic drawing, as revealed in the work of such artists as Jacquemart de Hesdin, shows the application of the earlier calligraphic movement and schematization of Villard de Honnecourt to a system of rhythmic, flamelike lines that, in their mannered, excited convolutions, impart a feeling of lightness and ghostly incorporeality to the sacred figures. Within this framework is a new feeling for realistic articulation, and the faces display the ecstatic, spiritual radiance of Gothic sculpture.

With the drawings of the Italian masters of the fourteenth century, we enter a new world of vision, a vision based on the awareness of classical antiquity and an awakening to nature. This is a vision based on seeing and observing, not on the repetition of earlier models from pattern books. It is as much a new language as the *dolce stil nuovo* of Dante and, in the same way, an Italian idiom based on the tradition of Latin poetry and realism. The compositions of Giotto and his followers are, of course, still dependent on fixed iconographical schemes, but the forms themselves, with their more organic construction and reliance on shading, take on a truly heroic sculpturesque appearance. Expressions, poses, and gestures, observed from life, introduce new qualities of drama and emotion—the new fervor of religious experience in human terms that we associate with St. Francis of Assisi. These figures move in a convincing spatial setting with massive dignity, like the ennobled idealizations of antiquity. There is in them a spirituality far more moving than the abstractions of the Romanesque and Byzantine because it is a spirituality realized in human terms.

These drawings belong to the proto-Renaissance that opened the way for the rebirth of nature, science, and classical form in the fifteenth century.

BENJAMIN ROWLAND, JR.

FOOTNOTES

1. *Drawing and Painting in Water Colours* (Dublin: printed by J. Potts, 1763), p. 1.

2. O. Sirén, *The Chinese on the Art of Painting* (Peiping, 1936), pp. 19–20.

3. M. Bucci, *Camposanto Monumentale di Pisa* (Pisa, 1960).

4. The caves of Altamira, some 30 km. west of Santander, were first noticed in 1868, and the paintings were discovered by Don Marcelino de Santuola in 1879. The paintings on the vaults of the cavern date from the Aurignacian through the Magdalenian periods. The technique of these decorations shows a progression from line engraving to a developed polychromatic rendering in the most recent examples.
   The caverns of Lascaux, first explored in 1940, are located near the village of Montignac-sur-Vézère. The wall paintings, which represent the high point of Magdalenian art, show a wide variety of techniques, including engraving and drawing with finger and brush. Owing to the deterioration of the paintings by exposure to the outside air, the caves were closed to the public in 1964.

5. The caves of Les Trois Frères and Tuc d'Audoubert are on the estates of the Comtes Bégouën near St. Giron in Ariège. They were first explored by the three sons of the distinguished historian Comte Henri Bégouën in 1912. We owe artistic and iconographical interpretation of these—as, indeed, the study of all the great paintings of the Ice Age—to the lifetime of research devoted to them by the greatest of all scholars in the field of prehistory, l'Abbé H. Breuil.

6. Sherman E. Lee, *A History of Far Eastern Art* (New York, 1964), p. 221, fig. 7; B. Rowland, *The Art and Architecture of India* (Harmondsworth, 1953 and 1956), pls. IV B and D.

7. The caves of Castillo are located 25 km. south of Santander, and their decorations consist entirely of engravings and drawings of the Aurignacian period.

8. Cf. J. Maringer and H.-G. Bandi, *Art in the Ice Age* (New York, 1953), p. 57, fig. 76.

9. Lee, *op. cit.*, pp. 310–11.

10. " All, however, agree that painting began with outlining a man's shadow. This was the first stage; in the second a single color was employed; and after the discovery of more elaborate methods this style which is still in vogue received the name of monochrome." Although from existing evidence of early painting it is impossible to demonstrate that the simple outline method actually preceded the mode of line and flat tone, Pliny's remarks emphasize the essentially draughtsmanly character of classical painting and the domination of contour drawings.

11. On these artists see *The Elder Pliny's Chapters on the History of Art,* trans. K. Gex-Blake (London, 1896).

12. The various examples of Athenian geometric vases are termed "Dipylon" from the double gate at Athens where they were discovered. They were dedicated as funeral monuments, and their painted decorations usually deal with the honors paid to the dead, although mythological subjects are occasionally included. See M. H. Swindler, *Ancient Painting* (New Haven, 1929), pp. 115 ff.

13. See H. W. Janson, *History of Art* (New York, n.d.), p. 301, fig. 460.

14. G. M. A. Richter, *The Sculpture and Sculptors of the Greeks* (New Haven, 1930), pl. 392; B. Rowland, *The Classical Tradition in Western Art* (Cambridge, 1963), figs. 6 and 7.

15. Rowland, *The Classical Tradition*... fig. 14.

16. See, for example, the drawings reproduced in M. Leiris, *Picasso and the Human Comedy* (New York: Modern Library, 1960).

17. B. Degenhart, "Autonome Zeichnungen bei Mittelalterlichen Künstlern," *Münchner Jahrbuch der Bildende Kunst,* III, 1 (1950), pp. 91 ff.

18. C. de Tolnay, *History and Technique of Old Master Drawings* (New York, 1943), p. 2.

19. R. Assunto, *La Critica d'Arte nel Pensiero mediovale* Milan, 1961), pp. 243 ff.

20. Swindler, *op. cit.,* figs. 541 and 542.

21. Cf. Janson, *op. cit.,* figs. 353–55.

22. Protean metamorphosis is referred to here as parallel to, not necessarily as an inspiration for, this type of Celtic ornament. Other references to such magical changes in bardic verse will be found in Davies, *The Rites and Mythology of the British Druids* (London, 1809).

23. H. R. Hahnloser, *Villard de Honnecourt* (Vienna, 1935), Taf. 48.

24. *Ibid.,* Taf. 43 and Abb. 139a.

25. Frederick II, *De Arte Venandi cum Avibus,* trans. as *The Art of Falconry* by C. A. Wood and M. Fyfe (Stanford, 1943).

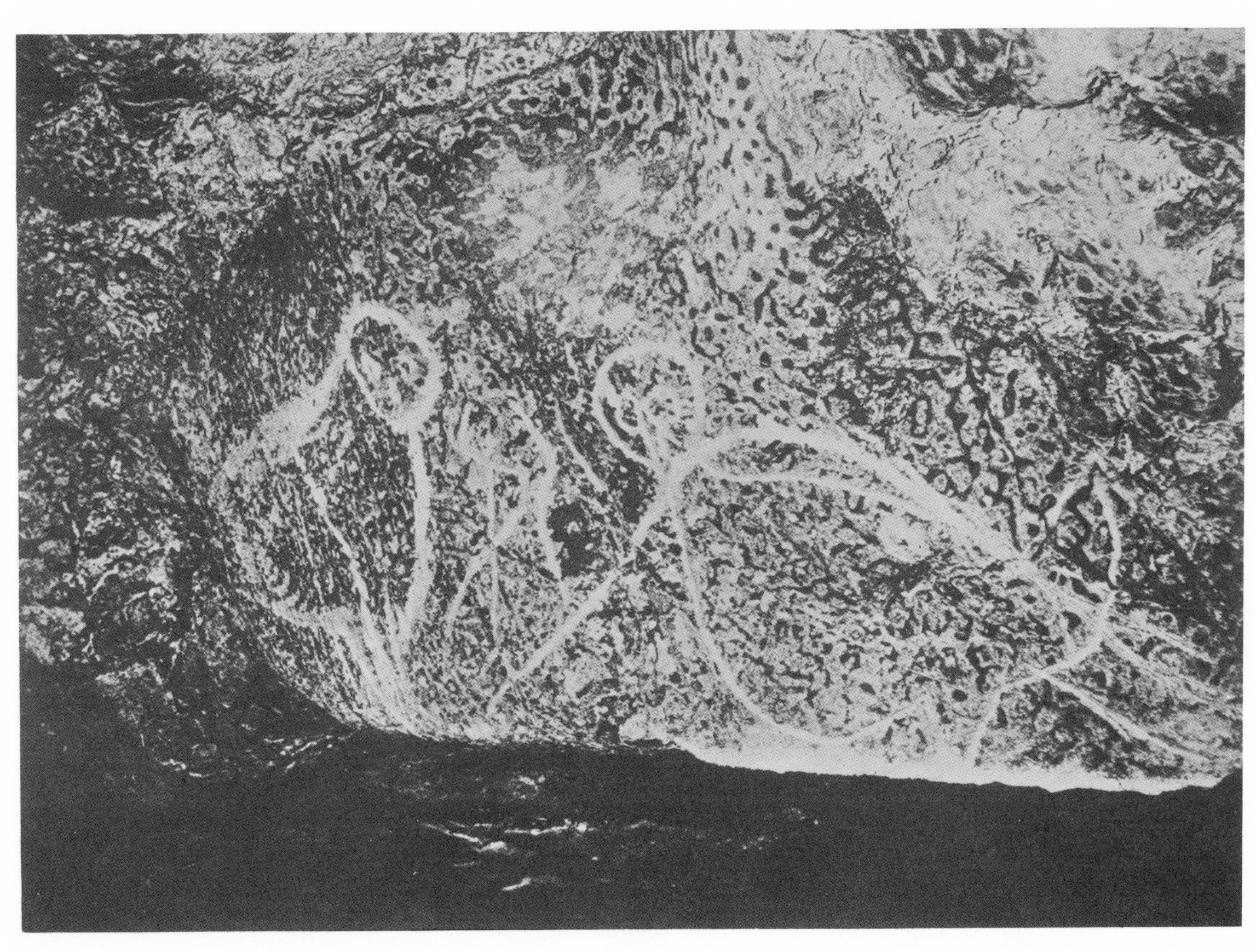

Plate 1

Owls and Chicks, Aurignacian period • engraving on stone, length 34½ inches • Cave of Les Trois Frères, Ariège

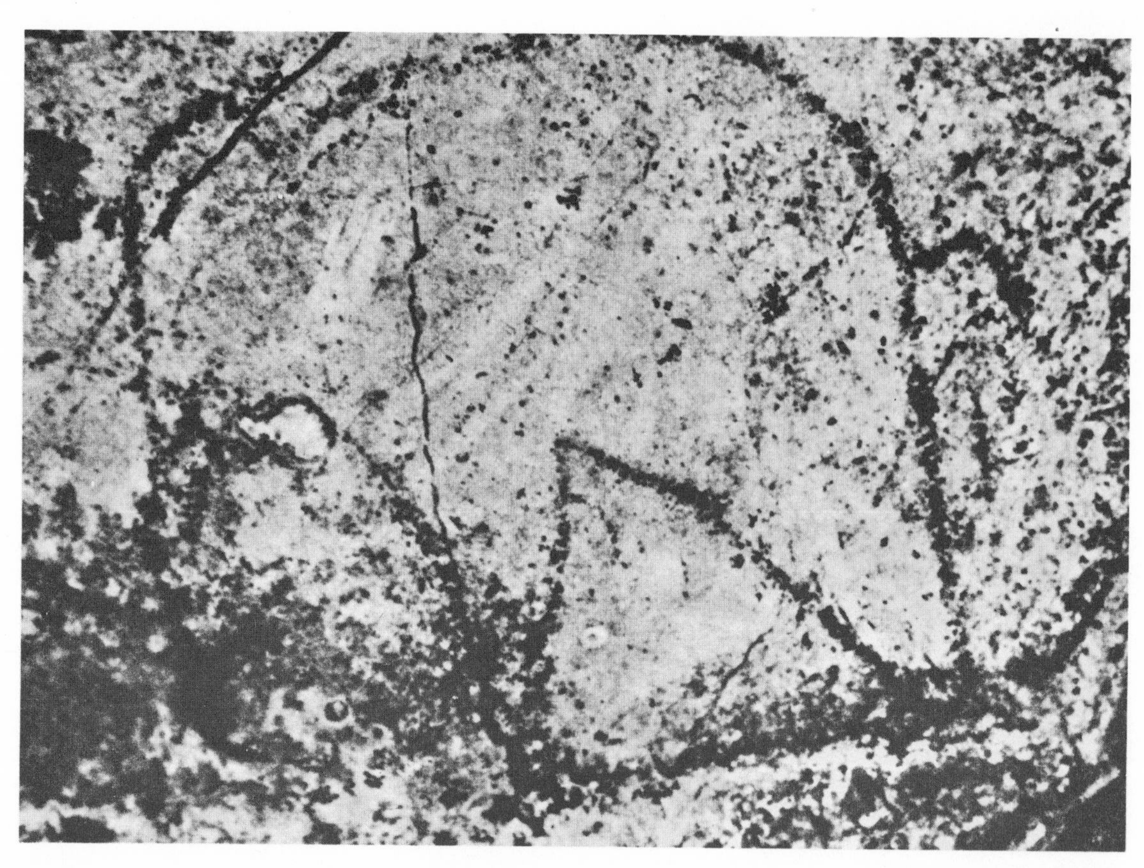

Plate 2

Elephant, Aurignacian period • cave painting, length 14⅛ inches • Castillo, Spain

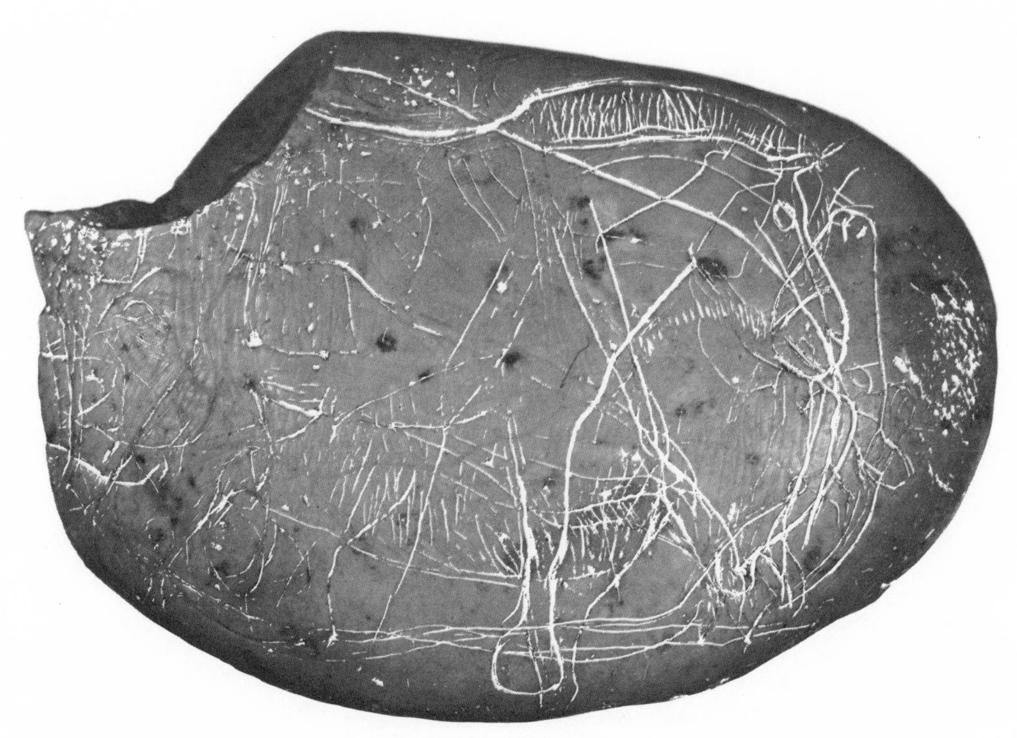

Plate 3

Animals, Magdalenian period • engraving on pebble from La Colombière, Ain, France
length 4¼ inches • Peabody Museum, Harvard University, Cambridge, Massachusetts

Plate 4

Stags and Salmon, early Magdalenian period • engraving on reindeer antler, 9⅝ inches • Cave of Lorthet, Hautes Pyrenées
Photo Courtesy of The American Museum of Natural History, New York

Plate 5

Recumbent Bison, Magdalenian period • cave painting, length 72 inches • Altamira, Spain

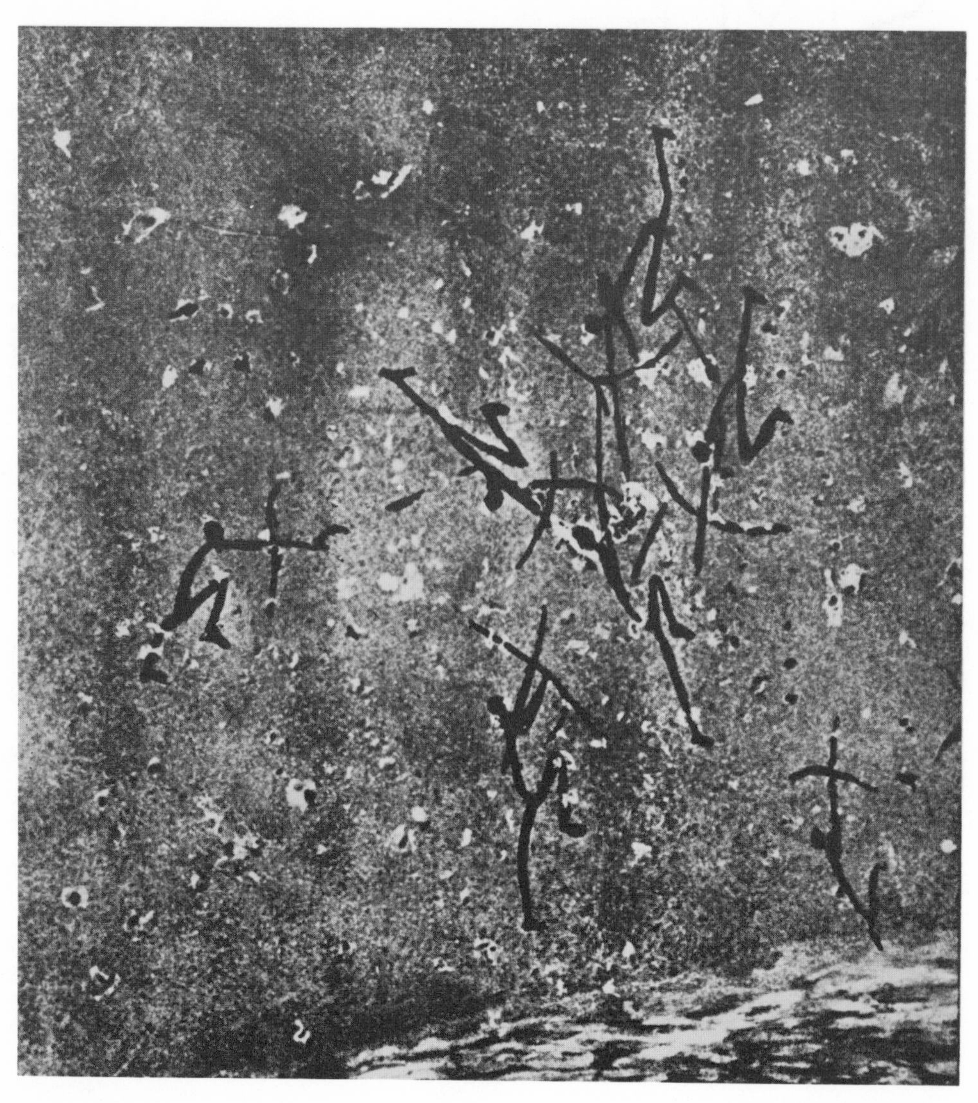

Plate 6

Archers Fighting, late Magdalenian period • cave painting, width 15¾ inches
Morella la Vella, Spain

Plate 7
Bison, Magdalenian period
engraving on limestone pebble
length 3 inches
La Genière, Ain, France

Plate 8

Standing Bison, Magdalenian period • cave painting, length 84 inches • Altamira, Spain

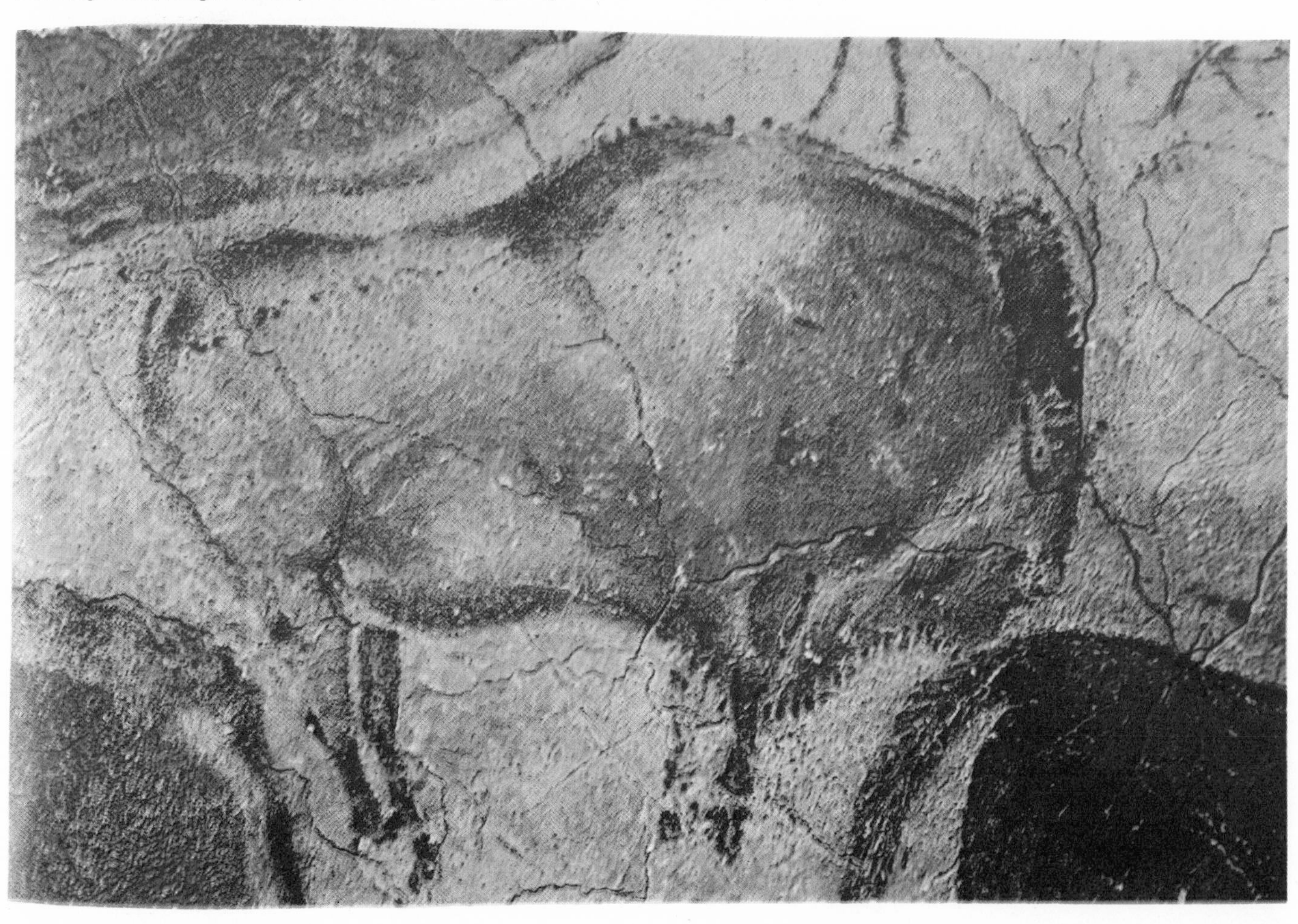

Plate 9

Deer, Magdalenian period • cave painting, length 89 inches • Altamira, Spain

Plate 10

Bull and Horses, Magdalenian period • cave painting • Lascaux Cave, France

Plate 11

Wounded Bison and Dead Hunter, Magdalenian period • cave painting, height 55 inches • Lascaux Cave, France

Plate 12

Horse, Magdalenian period • cave painting • Lascaux Cave, France

Plate 13

Bison, Magdalenian period • cave painting • Niaux, Ariège

Plate 14

Young Mammoth, Magdalenian period • cave painting • Peche-Merle, Lot

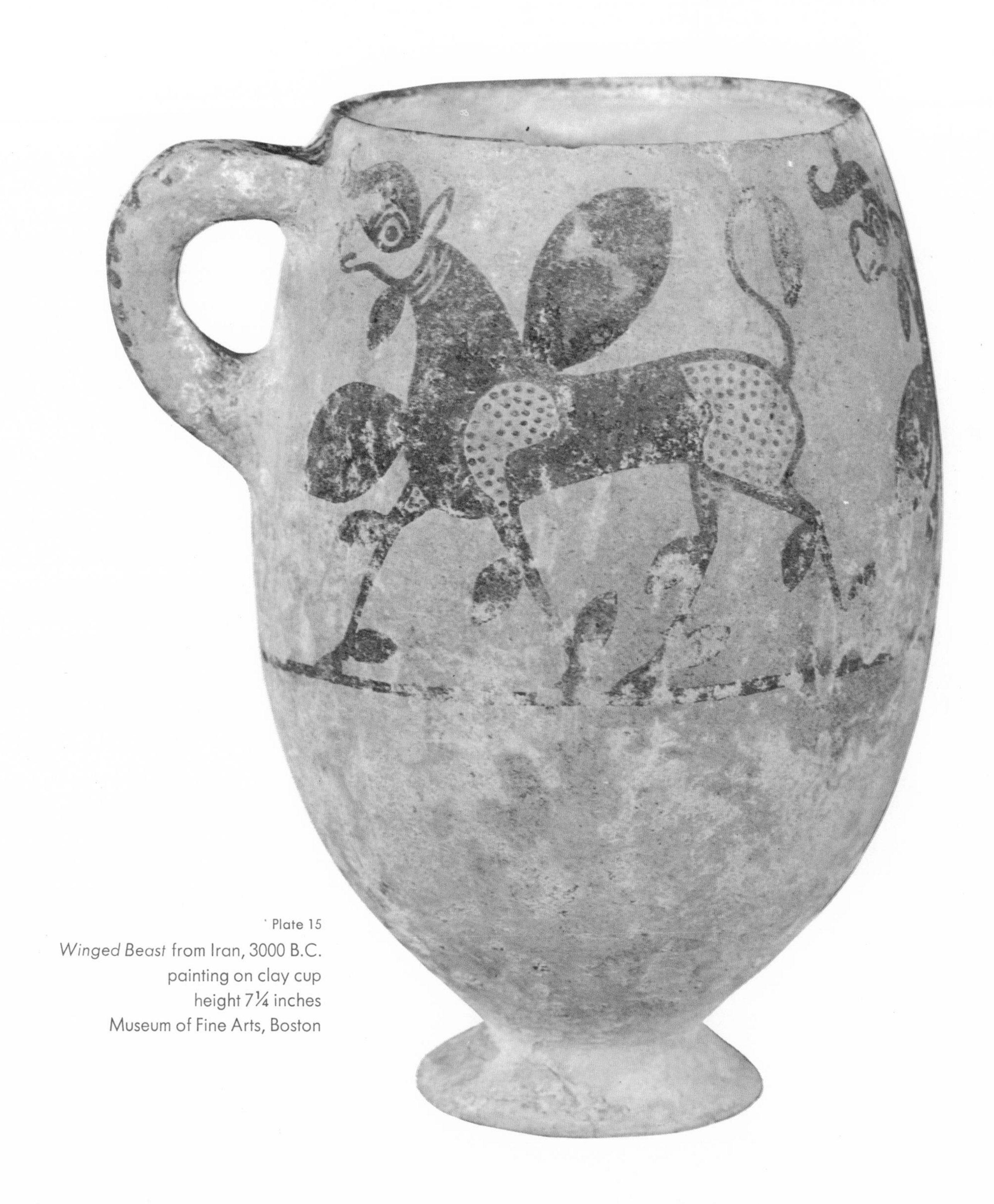

Plate 15

Winged Beast from Iran, 3000 B.C.
painting on clay cup
height 7¼ inches
Museum of Fine Arts, Boston

Plate 16

Mythological Beasts from Lagash
2800 B.C.
engraving on shell cup
height 2¾ inches
Louvre, Paris

Plate 17
Mythological Beasts from Tello,
2700 B.C.
engraving on silver and bronze
Vase of King Entemena
height 13¾ inches
Louvre, Paris

Plate 18

Winged Genius, from Til Barsip, 8th century B.C. • wall painting, 21¼ x 19½ inches • Louvre, Paris

Plate 19

Egyptian • *Wrestlers*, Dynasty XVIII (16th–15th century B.C.)
limestone, 4 13/16 x 5 3/4 inches • Aegyptische Abteilung, Staatliche Museen, Berlin

Plate 20
Bird (detail of *The Investiture of the King of Mari*) from the Palace of Mari
18th century B.C. • wall painting
Louvre, Paris

Plate 21
Ibex from Til Barsip, 8th century B.C. • wall painting • Louvre, Paris

Plate 22

Egyptian • *Head of Senmut*, Dynasty XVIII (16th–15th century B.C.) • ink on limestone
6¾ x 4 inches • The Metropolitan Museum of Art, New York, Anonymous Gift, 1931

Plate 23
Egyptian
Tumbling Girl
Dynasty XX (*ca.* 1180 B.C.)
painting on limestone
Soprintendenza Alle Antichità, Turin

Plate 24

Egyptian • *Weighing of the Heart of the Scribe Ani in the Afterlife, by the Gods Anubis and Thoth,* Dynasty XVIII (*ca.* 1450 B.C.) painted papyrus, 24 x 15⅛ inches • Courtesy of The Trustees of the British Museum, London

Plate 25

Egyptian • *A Cat Waiting Upon a Mouse*, Dynasty XIX (14th–13th century B.C.) • tempera on limestone, 3¾ x 6½ inches
Courtesy of The Brooklyn Museum

Plate 26

Rameses IV Slaying Prisoners, ca. 1160 B.C.
drawing on white limestone
11 15/16 x 7 7/8 inches
Museum of Fine Arts, Boston

Plate 27

Pharaoh in Chariot with Attendant
Dynasty XX (*ca.* 1160 B.C.)
drawing on white limestone
11 15/16 x 7 7/8 inches
Museum of Fine Arts, Boston

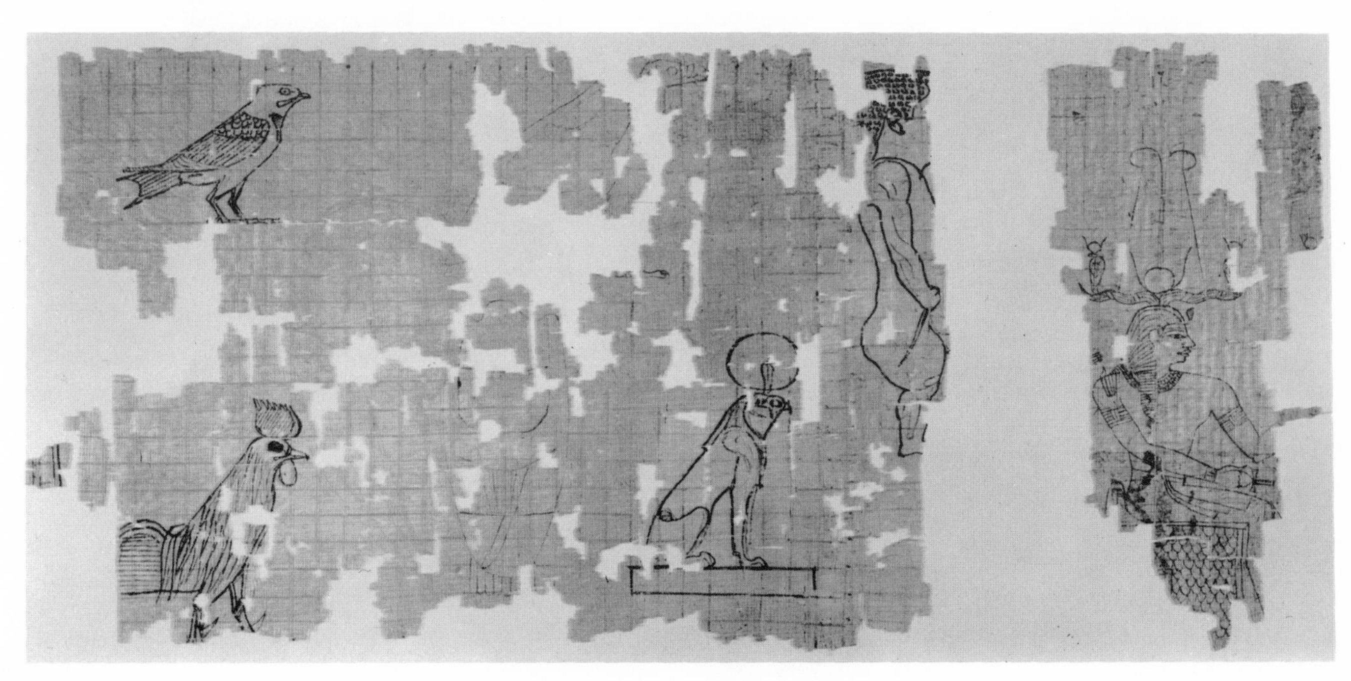

Plate 28

Preparatory Drawings, 1st century B.C. • ink on papyrus, left 9⅝ x 15 inches; right 9⅝ x 4½ inches
Papyrussammlung der Staatlichen Museum, Berlin

Plate 29
Prothesis ("Lying in State")
late 8th century B.C.
painting on sepulchral
Dipylon vase
height of detail 7⅞ inches
The Metropolitan Museum of Art
New York, Rogers Fund, 1914

Plate 30

KLITIAS and ERGOTIMOS
Legendary Scenes, the François Vase
ca. 550 B.C. • black-figured vase
height 26 inches
Soprintendenza Antichità D'Etruria
Florence

Plate 31

Heads, late 6th century B.C. • graffiti on limestone (fragment of relief at Palace of Darius, Persepolis, Iran)
length 6 inches • The Metropolitan Museum of Art, New York, Rogers Fund, 1914

Plate 32
LYDOS
Sons of the North Wind
6th century B.C.
black-figured painting
diameter 8⅝ inches
Courtesy of the
Fogg Art Museum
Harvard University
Cambridge, Massachusetts
Bequest, David M. Robinson

Plate 33

EXEKIAS

Dionysos in a Boat, 550–525 B.C.
black-figured *kylix*
diameter 13 inches
Antikensammlungen, Munich

Plate 34

A Scene of Combat, late 6th century B.C. • black-figured *oenochoe* with white ground • height 8 inches
Courtesy of the Fogg Art Museum
Harvard University
Cambridge, Massachusetts
Gift of Mr. E. P. Warren

Plate 35

EXEKIAS • *Achilles and Ajax Playing Draughts* (detail), late 6th century B.C. • black-figured *amphora*
full height 31¾ inches • Musei Vaticani, Rome

Plate 37
Triton, *ca.* 500 B.C.
white-ground painting
on cup fragment
Museum of Eleusis, Greece

Plate 36
EUPHRONIOS
Herakles and Antaios (detail)
late 6th century B.C.
red-figured *kylix*, height of frieze 7½ inches
Louvre, Paris

Plate 38

PEITHINOS • *Peleus and Thetis, ca.* 500 B.C. • red-figured painting on cup
diameter 8 11/16 inches • Antikenabteilung, Staatliche Museen, Berlin

Plate 39

DOURIS • *Satyr and Maenad, ca.* 475 B.C. • red-figured *kylix*
diameter of *kylix* 11 5/8 inches • Courtesy of the Fogg Art Museum
Harvard University, Cambridge, Massachusetts • Bequest of Joseph C. Hoppin

Plate 40

Apollo and Nymph, 475–450 B.C.
white-ground *kylix*
diameter 4 9/16 inches
Museum of Fine Arts, Boston

Plate 41

HIERON and MAKRON • *Dancing Maenads and Herm of Dionysos*, 490–480 B.C.
red-figured painting on cup, height of figures 4 9/16 inches • Antikenabteilung, Staatliche Museen, Berlin

Plate 42

SOSIAS • *Achilles and Patroclus*
ca. 480 B.C.
red-figured painting on cup
diameter 7 inches
Antikenabteilung
Staatliche Museen, Berlin

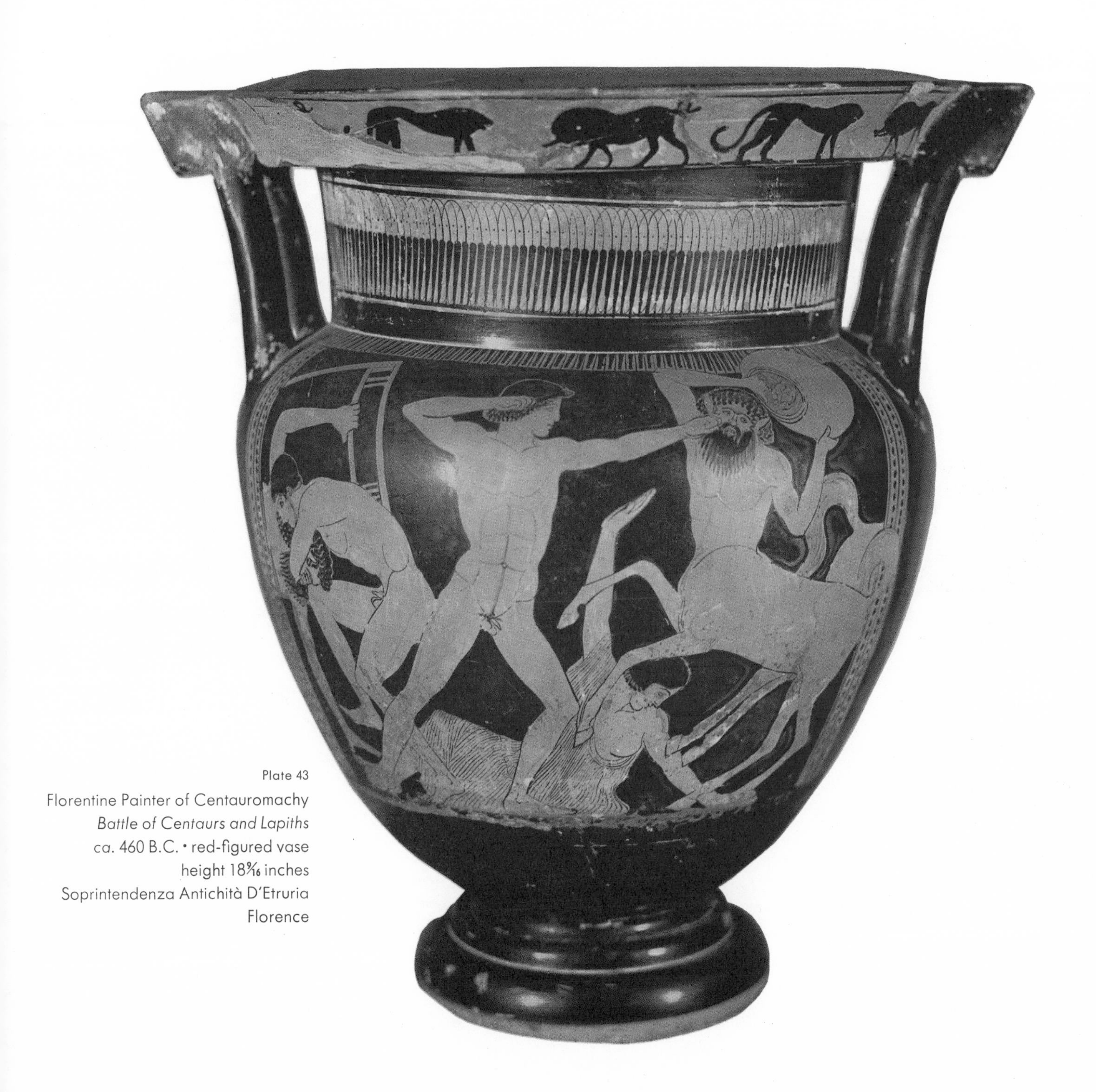

Plate 43
Florentine Painter of Centauromachy
Battle of Centaurs and Lapiths
ca. 460 B.C. • red-figured vase
height 18⁹⁄₁₆ inches
Soprintendenza Antichità D'Etruria
Florence

Plate 44

Aphrodite Riding a Goose, 475–450 B.C. • white-ground clay cup, diameter 9⁷⁄₁₆ inches • Courtesy of the Trustees of the British Museum, London

Plate 45

Penthesilea Painter • *Achilles Slaying Penthesilea*
ca. 460 B.C. • red-figured *kylix*, diameter 18⅛ inches
Antikensammlungen, Munich

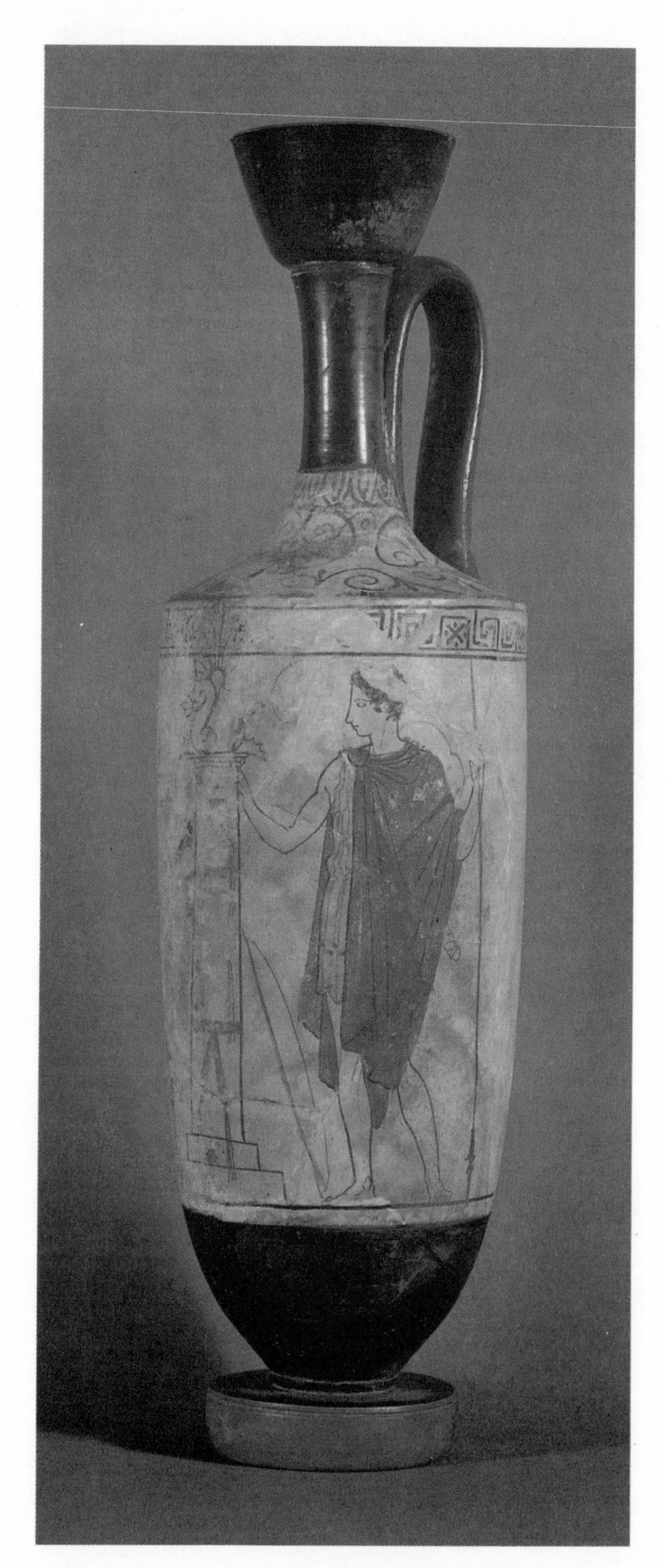

Plate 46
Offering at a Tomb, 450–400 B.C.
white-ground *lekythos*
height 14¾ inches
Courtesy of the Fogg Art Museum
Harvard University
Cambridge, Massachusetts
Bequest of Henry W. Haynes

Plate 47

Woman by a Tomb, ca. 440 B.C.
white-ground *lekythos*
height 7 1/16 inches
Antikensammlungen, Munich

Plate 48
Niobid Painter
Death of the Niobids, *ca.* 450 B.C.
red-figured painting on vase
Louvre, Paris

Plate 49

Athena and Aphrodite, 450–400 B.C. • drawing on ivory
State Hermitage, Leningrad

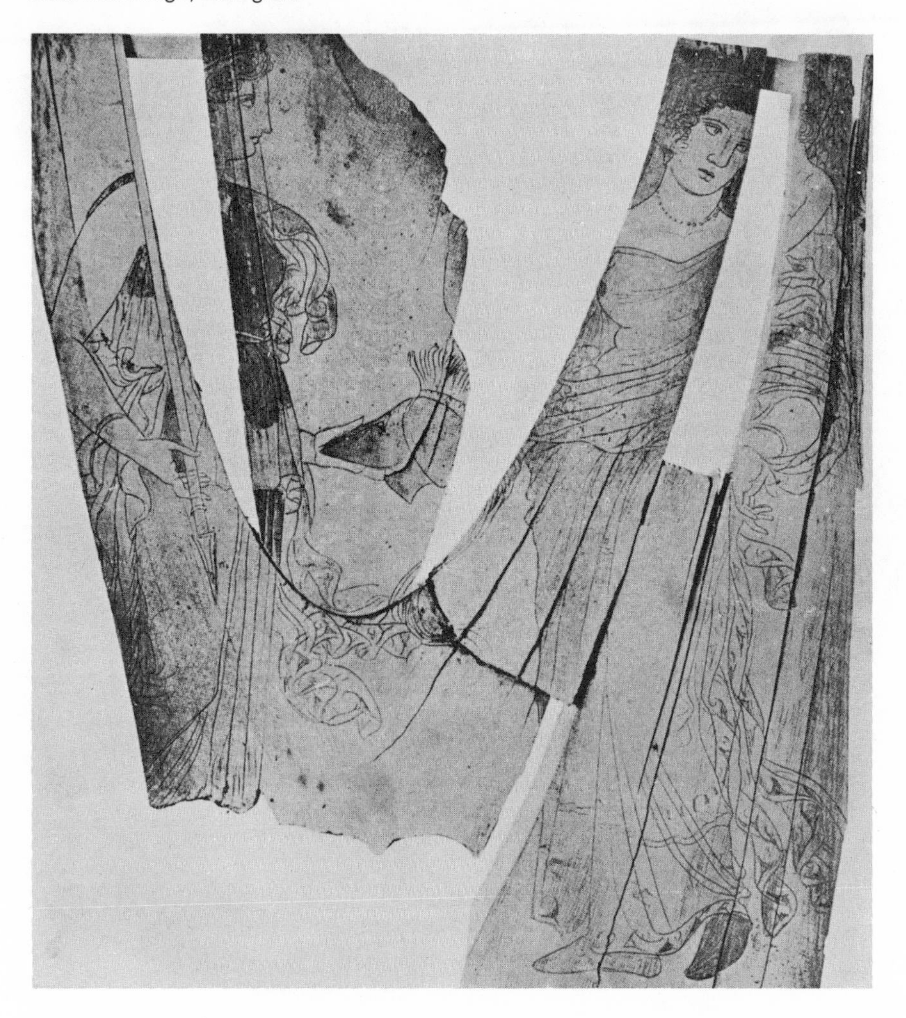

Plate 50

ARISTOPHANES and ERGINOS • *Herakles, Nessus, and Deianeira, ca.* 420 B.C. • red-figured *kylix*
Museum of Fine Arts, Boston

Plate 51

Etruscan • *Pan and Aphrodite*, 4th century B.C. • bronze mirror
diameter 7¼ inches • Courtesy of the Trustees of the British Museum, London

Plate 53

Cupid and Psyche, *ca.* 100 A.D.
ink, on papyrus, 9⅞ x 5⅞ inches
Soprintendenza Antichità D'Etruria
Florence

Plate 52

Peirithoos, Hippodameia, and the Centaur Eurytion (copy of a painting attributed to Zeuxis, 4th century B.C.), 1st century A.D.
painting on marble, width 17¾ inches
Museo Nazionale, Naples

Plate 54

Graeco-Roman • *Knucklebone Players,* 1st Century A.D. • painting on marble • Museo Nazionale, Naples

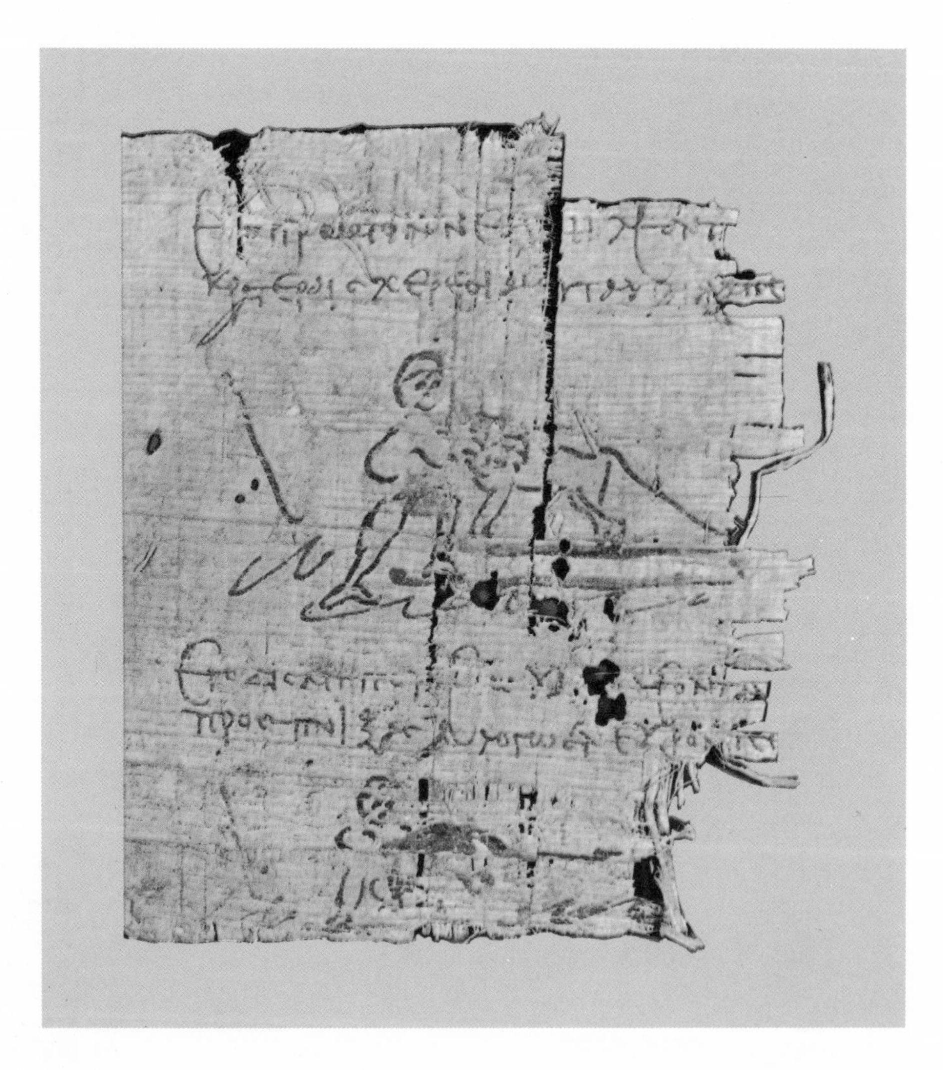

Plate 55

Herakles and the Nemean Lion
3rd century A.D. • ink on papyrus
1⅜ x 2³⁄₁₆ inches
Ashmolean Museum, Oxford

Plate 56

Briseis and the Heralds, 4th century A.D. • ink on papyrus, 5 3/16 x 5 11/16 inches • Bayerische Staatsbibliothek, Munich

Plate 57

Early Christian • *Christ and His Disciples on Lake Tiberius*, 5th century A.D. • ink on papyrus, 8⅝ x 3$^{15}/_{16}$ inches
Soprintendenza Antichità D'Etruria, Florence

Plate 58

Surveyor, 6th century A.D.
pen and ink on parchment
$12\frac{7}{16}$ x $9\frac{5}{8}$ inches
Herzog August Bibliothek
Wolfenbüttel

Plate 59

St. Mark from St. Chad's Gospel
ca. 720 A.D. • pen and ink and color
on parchment, $8\frac{1}{16}$ x $11\frac{13}{16}$ inches
Courtesy of the Dean and Chapter
Litchfield Cathedral, Staffordshire

Plate 60

Irish Celtic
Chi-Ro, Initial page of the Gospel
of St. Matthew from the *Book of Kells*
early 9th century A.D.
ink and color on vellum
13 x $9\frac{1}{2}$ inches
By Permission of the
Board of Trinity College, Dublin

h generatio

Plate 61

Irish Celtic
St. Mark's Lion from the *Book of Armagh*, 807 A.D. • ink on vellum
7½ x 8½ inches
By Permission of the Board of Trinity College, Dublin

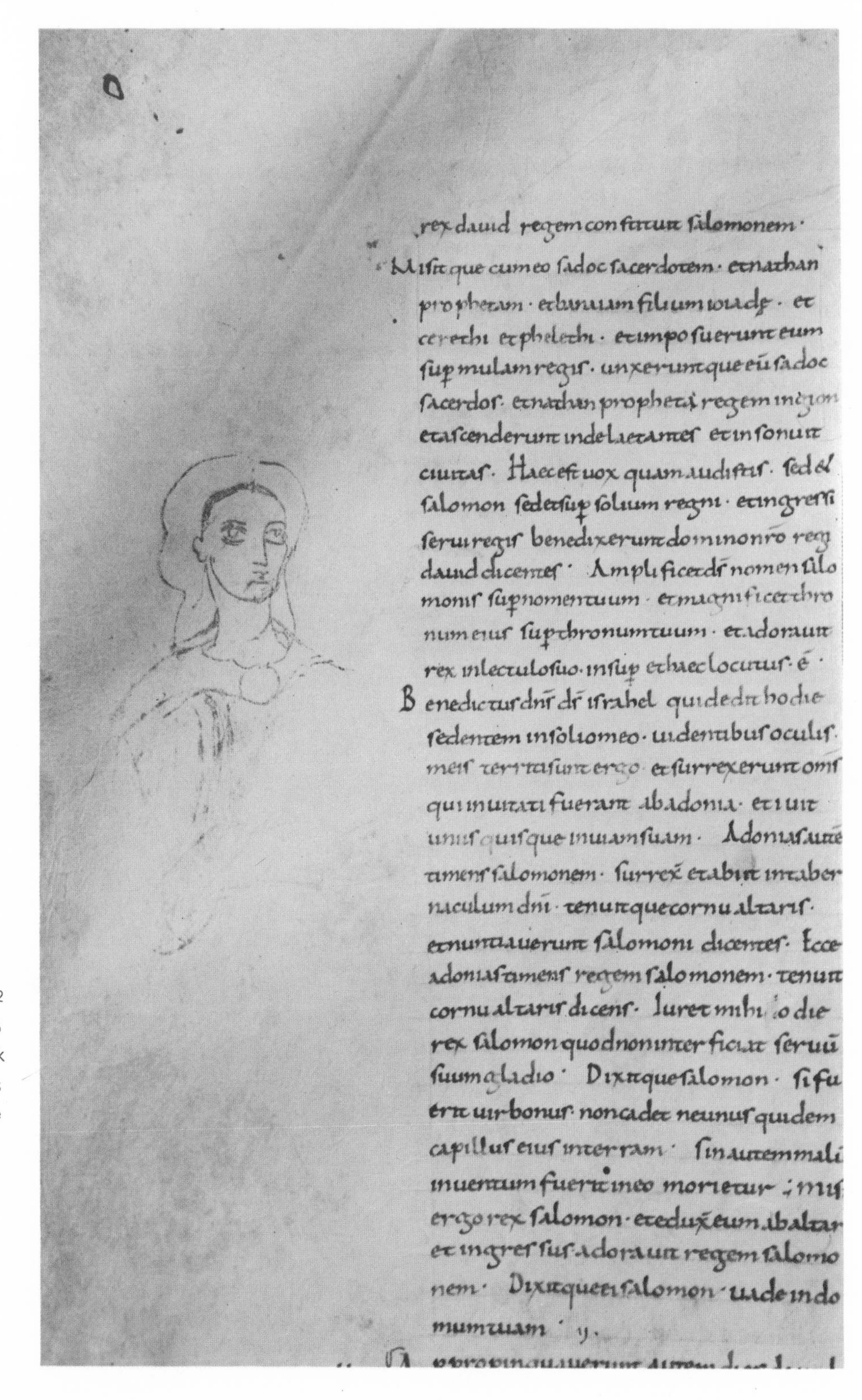

Plate 62

Female Figure or Saint from ms. B6
9th century A.D. • pen and ink
3⅛ x 2 inches
Biblioteca Vallicelliana, Rome

Plate 63

St. John from ms. B25
9th century A.D. • pen and ink
$7\frac{1}{2} \times 5\frac{5}{16}$ inches
Biblioteca Vallicelliana, Rome

Plate 64
Carolingian
St. Matthew from the Ebbo Gospels
825 A.D. • gouache
7½ x 5½ inches
Municipal Library, Epernay

QUARETRISTISESANIMA
MEA ETQUARECONTUR
BASME;
SPERAINDOQMADHUC
CONFITEBORILLI·SALU
TAREUULTUSMEIETDSMS;
XLII PSALMUS DAUID
IUDICAMEDSET
DISCERNECAUSAMMEAM
DEGENTENONSCA ABHOMI
NEINIQUOETDOLOSOERU
EME;
QUIATUESDSFORTITUDO
MEA·QUAREMEREPPULIS
TIETQUARETRISTISINCEDO
DUMADFLIGITMEINIMICUS
EMITTELUCEMTUAMETUERI
TATEMTUAM IPSAMEDEDU
XERUNTETADDUXERIN
MONTEMSCMTUU ETIN
TABERNACULATUA;
ETINTROIBOADALTAREDI
ADDMQUILAETIFICAT
IUUENTUTEMMEAM;
CONFITEBORTIBIINCI
THARADSDSMEUS·
QUARETRISTISESANIMA
MEAETQUARECONTUR
BASME;
SPERAINDOQNMADHUC
CONFITEBORILLI·SALU
TAREUULTUSMEIETDSMS

Plate 65

Carolingian • Illustration of Psalm 42 from the Utrecht Psalter, 825–50 A.D. • pen and ink on parchment
12 13/16 x 10 inches • University Library, Utrecht

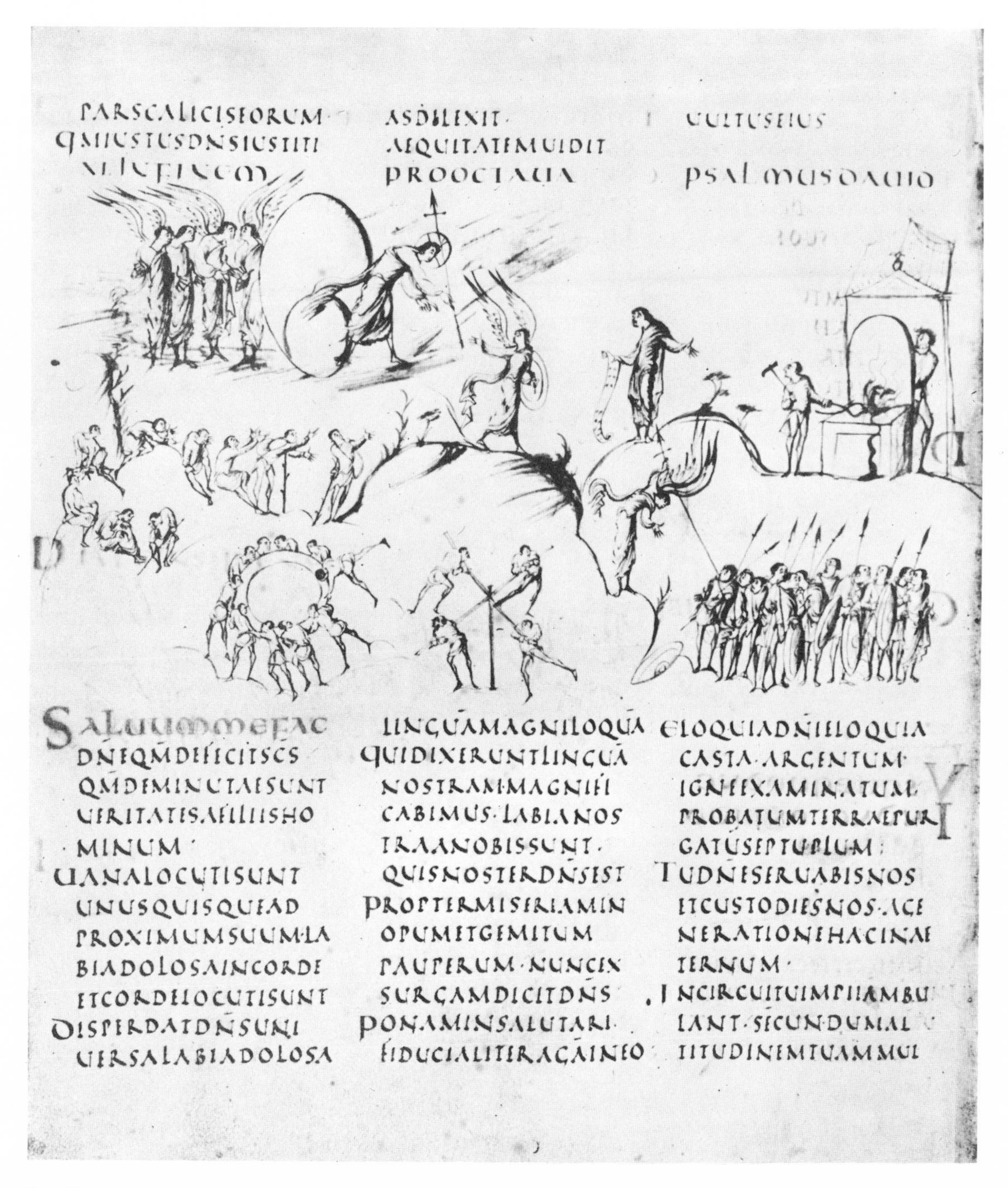

Plate 66

Carolingian • Illustration of Psalm 12 from the Utrecht Psalter, 825–50 A.D. • pen and ink on parchment
12$^{13}/_{16}$ x 10 inches • University Library, Utrecht

Plate 67

School of Canterbury • Illustration from Harley Psalter, *ca.* 1000 A.D. • pen and ink, *ca.* 10 x 4½ inches
Courtesy of the Trustees of the British Museum, London

Plate 68

Winchester School
Crucifixion from Harley ms. 2904
late 10th century A.D. • pen and ink and color
13⅛ x 9⅛ inches
Courtesy of the Trustees of the British Museum
London

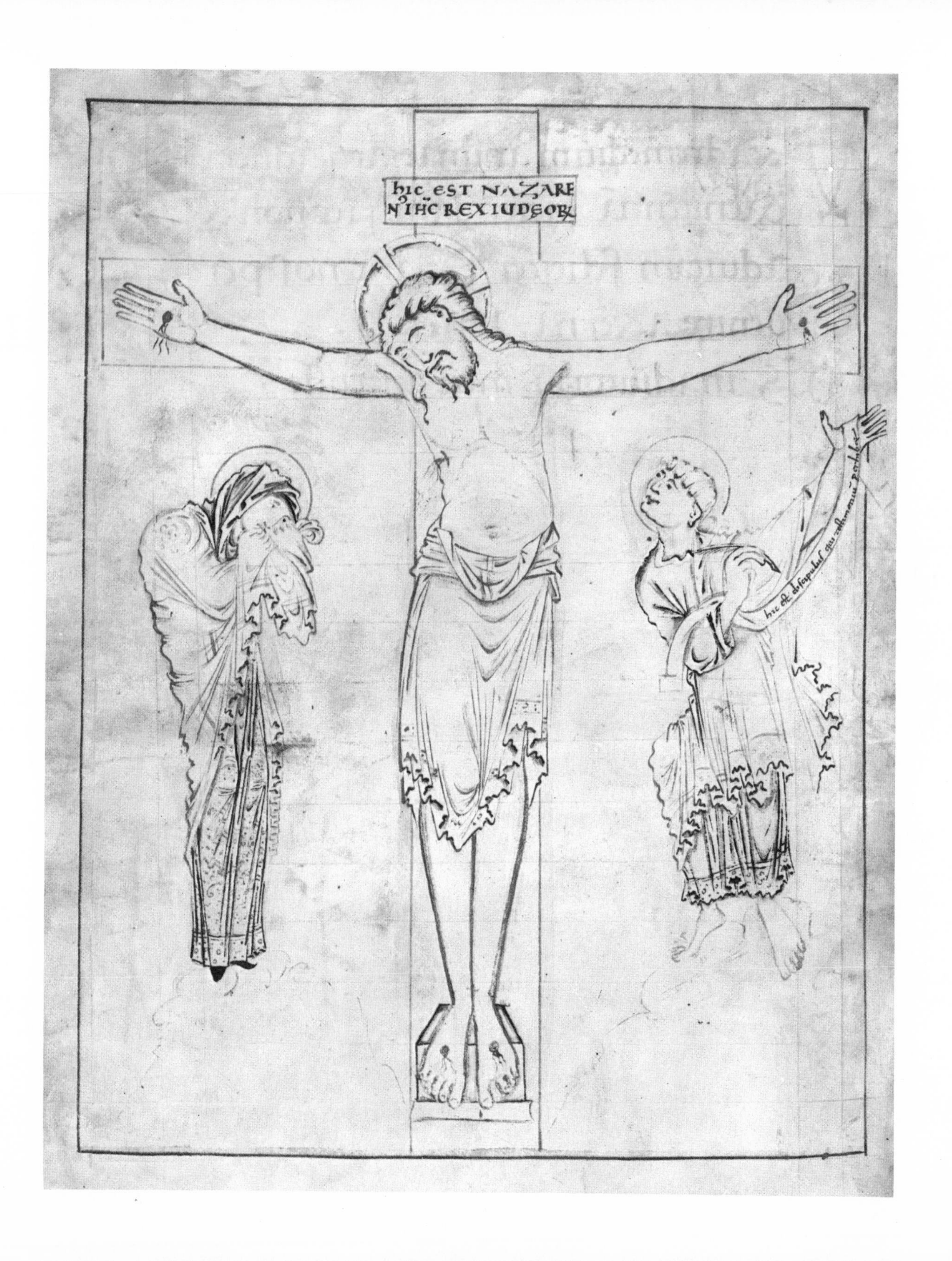
HIC EST NAZARE
N IHC REX IUDEOR

Plate 69

Southern Italian

Annunciation, from ms. 99,

11th century A.D. • pen and ink

13¼ x 9⅞ inches

Archivio di Montecassino

Plate 70
Italian
Fabulous Monster from the *Commentary of St. Jerome*
11th century A.D. • pen and ink
Archivio di Montecassino

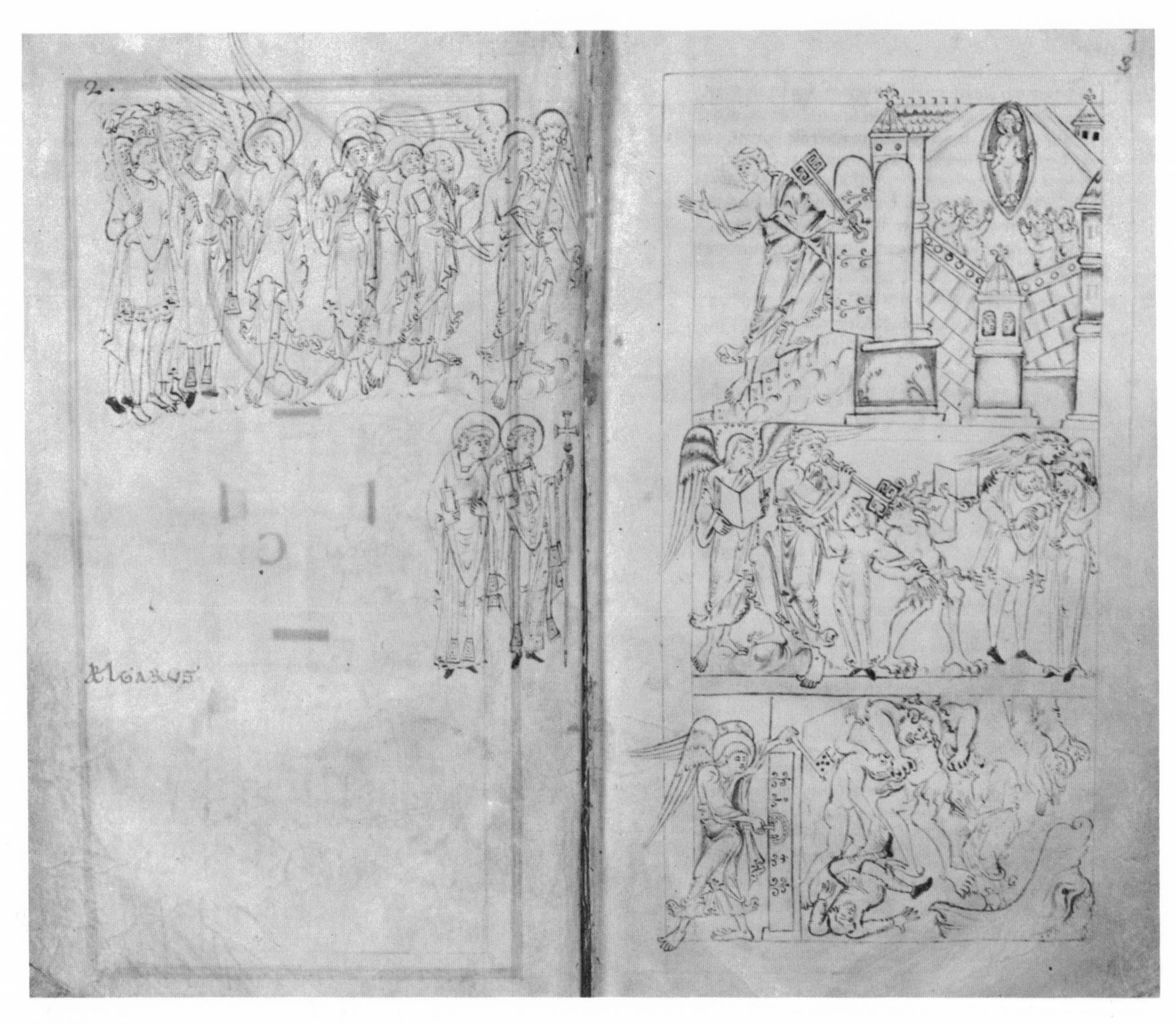

Plate 71

English • *Last Judgment* from Stowe ms. 944, *ca.* 1020 A.D. • pen and ink, 10 x 11 inches
Courtesy of the Trustees of the British Museum, London

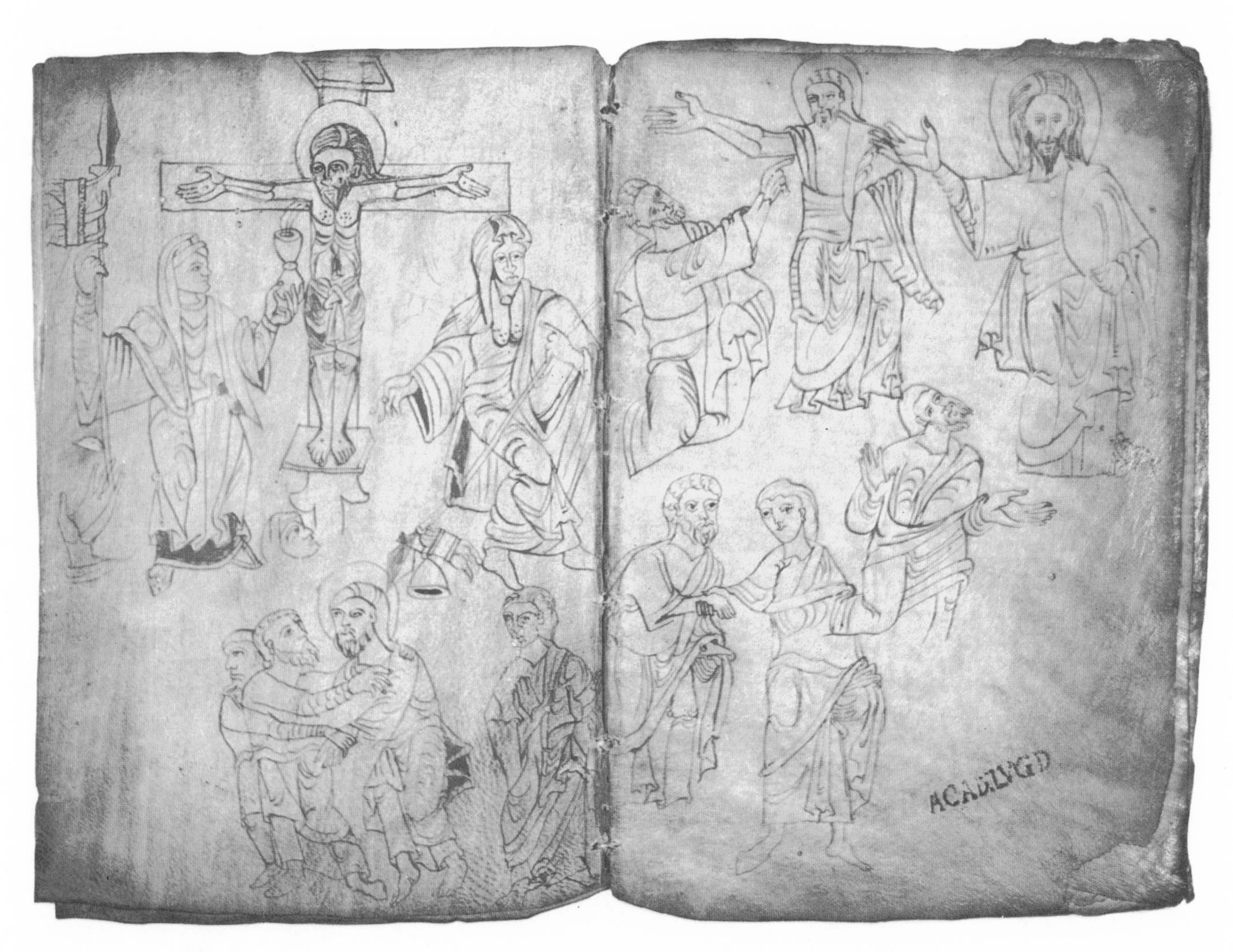

Plate 72

Ademar de CHABANNES • Illustration from Prudentius ms., *ca.* 1025 A.D. • pen and ink on parchment, $8\frac{5}{16}$ x $5\frac{3}{4}$ inches
University Library, Leiden

Plate 73

Byzantine Master

Drawing of a Saint, 11th century A.D.

pen and ink

Bibliothèque Nationale, Paris

[illegible] ECCLAE

Dicebat autem et parab[illegible] ad
illos quoniam oportet illos semper
orare et non deficere. Dicit apostolus:
Semper gaudete, sine intermissione
orate. Quis autem potest ita semp[er]
orare ut nunquam deficiat vel inter mis-
sione precibus insistere [illegible]
[illegible] aut dormiendi
tempus habeat. Aut ergo dicendum
est cum semper orare et non deficere quia canonicis horis [illegible]
[illegible] ecclesiastice traditionis
psalmo diis precibus q[ue] consuetis
dominum laudare et rogare non
desistat et hoc esse quod psalmista
dicebat: Benedicam dominum in omni
tempore, semper laus eius in ore
meo. Aut certe omnia quae iustus secundum deum gerit ad
orationem esse reputanda. Quia
enim iustus sine intermissione
quae iusta sunt agit, per hoc sine intermissione iustus orabit. Nec
umquam sine oratione cessabit
nisi iustus esse desistat. Iudex
quidem erat in quadam civitate
qui dominum non timebat et
hominem non reverebatur. Vidua autem quaedam erat in civitate
illa et veniebat ad eum dicens:
Vindica me de adversario meo. Et
nole[bat]. Post haec autem dixit intra se:
Et si deum non timeo nec hominem
revereor, tamen quia molesta est
mihi haec vidua, vindicabo illam,
ne in novissime veniens suggil-
let me. Parabolas dominus aut secundum
similitudinem aliquam ponit, sicut
de homine qui habebat duos filios,
maiorem in agro sibi propinquan-
tem, Minorem autem in propin-
quo luxuriantem; aut ex ipsa dis-
similitudine aliquid probat, velut
est illud: Quod si foenum agri
quod hodie est et cras in clibanum [illegible]

Plate 74

Northern French

Trinity and St. George from Anchin

late 11th century A.D.

pen and ink on vellum

15 x 6½ inches

Private Collection

Cambridge, Massachusetts

Plate 75

Byzantine Master

St. Luke, 11th century A.D.

pen and ink on vellum

$10\frac{5}{8}$ x 8 inches

Private Collection

Cambridge, Massachusetts

Plate 76

Northern Italian

Dancer from ms. A1/1

12th century A.D. • pen and ink

$2\frac{3}{16}$ x $1\frac{3}{16}$ inches

Biblioteca Vallicelliana, Rome

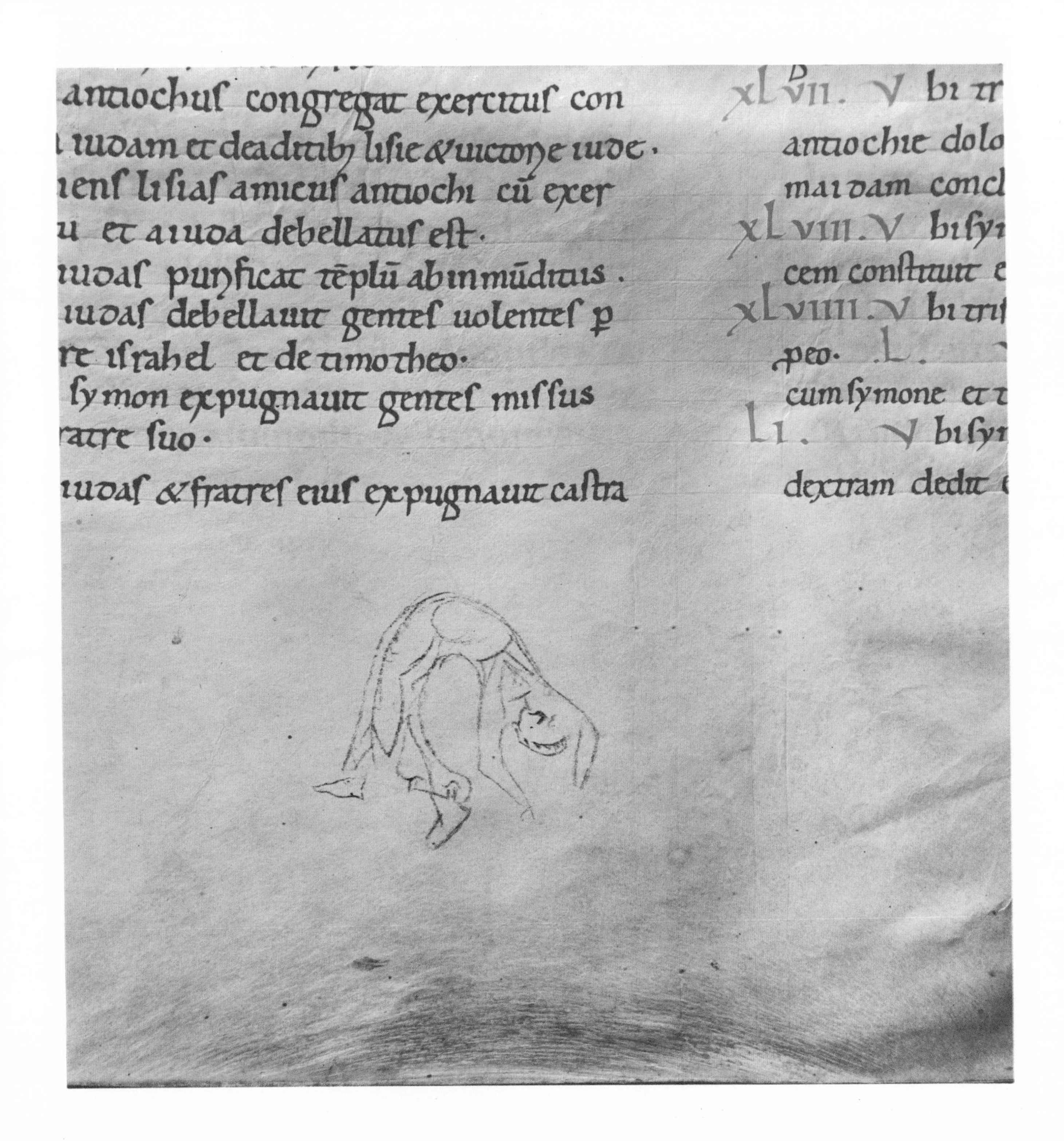
antiochus congregat exercitus con
iudam et de aditib; lisie & uictorie iude.
iens lisias amicus antiochi cū exer
u et a iuda debellatus est.
iudas purificat tēplū ab inmūditiis.
iudas debellauit gentes uolentes p
re israhel et de timotheo.
symon expugnauit gentes missus
ratre suo.
iudas & fratres eius expugnauit castra

XLVII. V bi tr
antiochie dolo
mai dam concl
XLVIII. V bisyr
cem constituit e
XLVIIII. V bi tris
peo. L.
cum symone et t
LI. V bisyr
dextram dedit

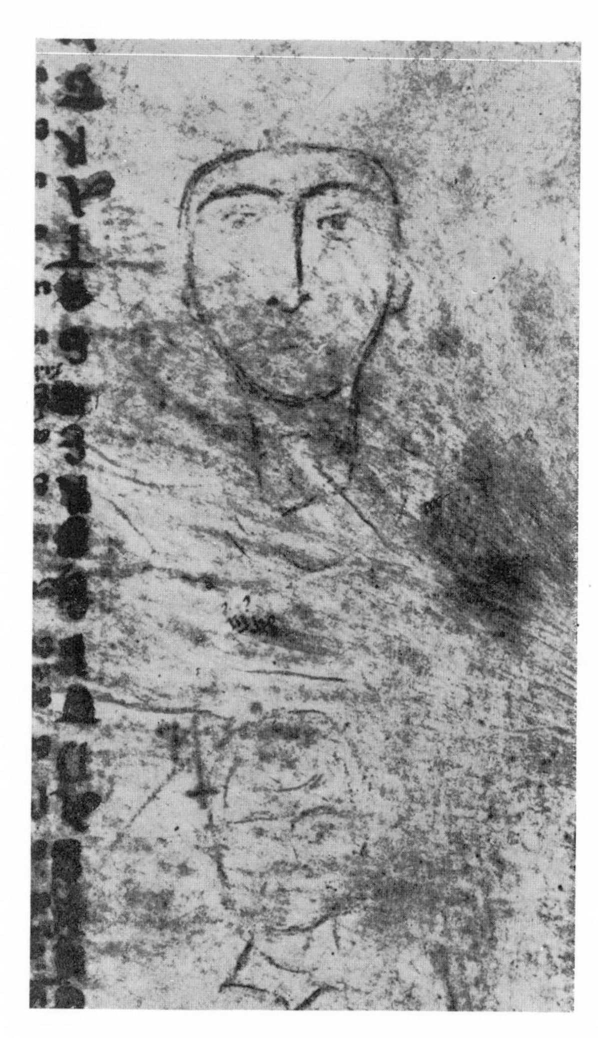

Plate 77

Italian · *Madonna and Child* from ms. Reg. lat. 2090
11th–13th century A.D. · pen and ink · 5 1/16 x 2 15/16 inches
Biblioteca Vaticana, Rome

Plate 78

Italian · *St. Francis,* from ms. Reg. lat. 2090
11th–13th century A.D.
pen and ink · Biblioteca Vaticana, Rome

Plate 79
Italian
Christ Enthroned with Saints and Donors from ms. Cod. 3.210, 1104 A.D.
sepia and yellowish glue
12⅛ x 8⅝ inches
Biblioteca Piana, Cesena

Plate 80
Italian
Portrait of Frederick II, frontispiece from ms. Pal. lat. 1071
13th century A.D.
pen and ink and color
Biblioteca Vaticana, Rome

Plate 81
Italian
Owls and Hawks from ms. Pal. lat. 1071, 13th century A.D.
pen and ink and color
Biblioteca Vaticana, Rome

Plate 82

Villard de HONNECOURT • *Drawings of Antique Statues*, from ms. fr. 19093, ca. 1225–50 A.D. • leadpoint reinforced with pen lines on parchment, 5 15/16 x 9 1/16 inches • Bibliothèque Nationale, Paris

Plate 83

Villard de HONNECOURT • *Lion*, from ms. fr. 19093, *ca.* 1225–50 A.D. • leadpoint reinforced with pen lines on parchment, $9\frac{1}{16} \times 5\frac{15}{16}$ inches • Bibliothèque Nationale, Paris

Plate 84

Villard de HONNECOURT • *Two Saints*, from ms. fr. 19093, *ca.* 1225–50 A.D. • leadpoint reinforced with pen lines on parchment, $9\frac{1}{16} \times 5\frac{15}{16}$ inches • Bibliothèque Nationale, Paris

Plate 85
German
Title Page from Bede ms.
12th century A.D.
pen and ink on vellum
11⅞ x 8¼ inches
Private Collection
Cambridge, Massachusetts

Plate 86

Italian • *Falconers*, from ms. Pal. lat. 1071, 13th century A.D. • pen and ink underdrawing
Biblioteca Vaticana, Rome

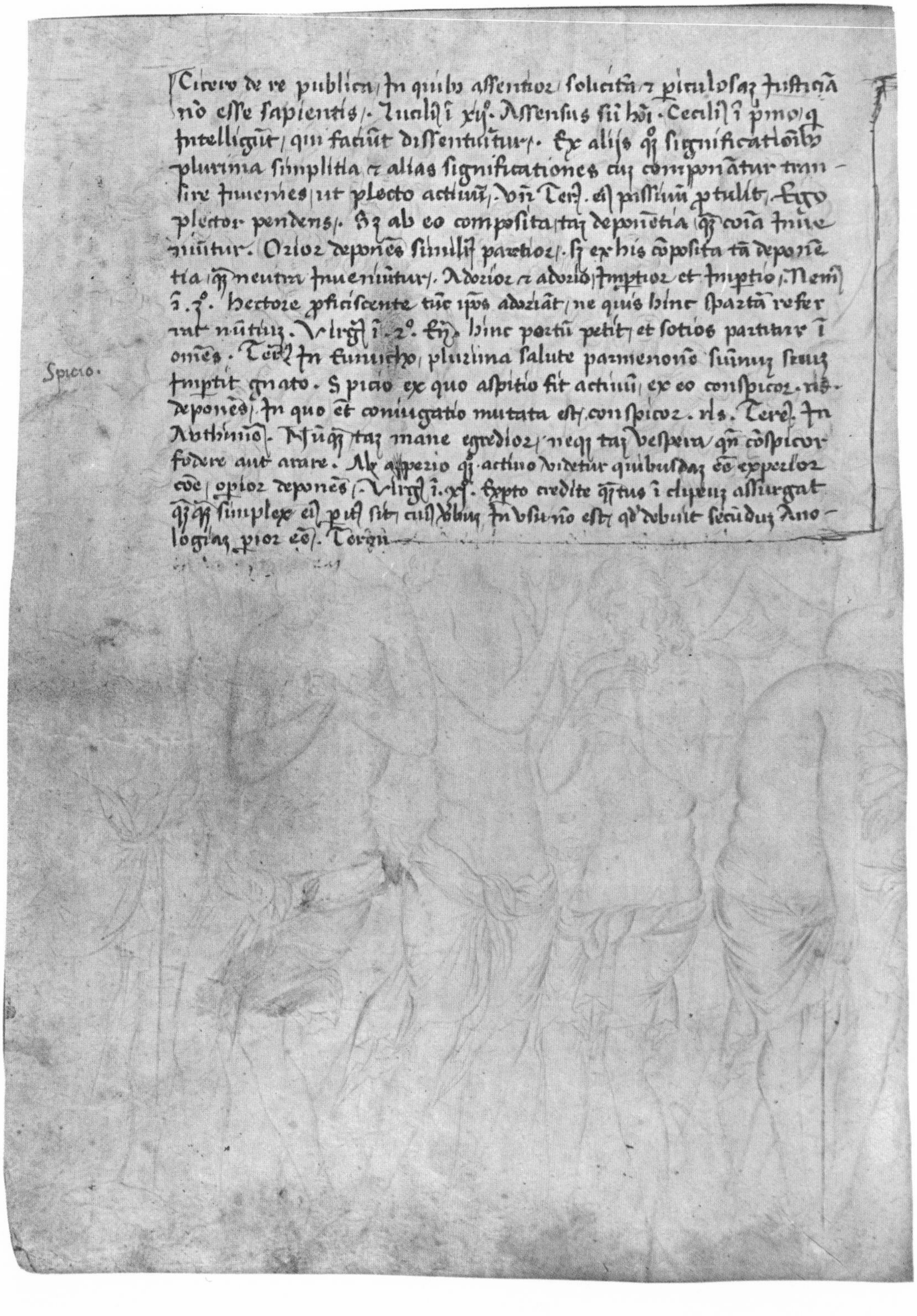

Cicero de re publica, in quibus assentior sollicitam et periculosam iustitiam
non esse sapientis. [illegible] xii. Assensus sum homini. Cecilius in primo quod
intelligunt qui faciunt dissentiuntur. Ex aliis que significationibus
plurima simplicia et alias significationes cum componantur tran-
sire invenies, ut plecto activum, unde Terentius eius passivum protulit. Ergo
plector pendens. Sed ab eo composita tam deponentia quam communia inveniuntur. Ordior deponens similiter partior. Sed ex his composita tam deponentia quam neutra inveniuntur. Adorior et adorio, impertior et impertio. [illegible]
in .3°. Hectore proficiscente tunc ipsos adoriatur ne quis hinc Sparta refer-
at nuntium. Virgilius in .2°. [illegible] hinc portum petit et socios partitur in
omnes. Terentius in Eunucho, plurima salute Parmenonem summum suum
impertit Gnato. Spicio ex quo aspicio fit activum, ex eo conspicor, aris
deponens, in quo et coniugatio mutata est, conspicor, aris. Terentius in
[illegible]. Neque tam mane egredior neque tam vespera quin conspicor
fodere aut arare. Ab aperio quod activum videtur quibusdam est experior
eius, opperior deponens. Virgilius in .xi. Experto credite quantus in clipeum assurgat
quam quam simplex eius [illegible] sit, cuius verbum in usu non est, quod debuit secundum ana-
logiam perior esse. Terentius

Spicio.

Plate 87

Italian

Forty Martyrs from ms. Barb. lat. 144

13th century A.D. • pen and ink

Biblioteca Vaticana, Rome

Plate 88

Italian

Illustration from the Bible of Farfa

ms. Vat. lat. 5729, 13th century A.D.

pen and ink

Biblioteca Vaticana, Rome

Plate 89

Austrian Master • *The Flight into Egypt and the Baptism of Christ, ca.* 1320 A.D. • pen in red and India ink, pen and brush in watercolors and gouache, white body color on vellum, 8 13/16 x 14 3/4 and 15 1/2 inches (irregular) • Albertina, Vienna

Plate 90

Giusto di MENABUOI (?) • *Joseph Cast into the Pit by His Brethren*, late 14th century A.D. • brush on grounded vellum heightened with gouache, $6\frac{15}{16} \times 9\frac{1}{2}$ inches • Victoria and Albert Museum, London

Plate 91

The Body of Light (Corpus Fulgidum) from the *Autobiography* of Opicinus de Canistris, 14th century A.D.
metal stylus and pen and ink
Biblioteca Vaticana, Rome

Plate 92

Florentine • *The Visitation*, early 15th century A.D. • pen and bistre on parchment, 8 1/16 x 12 7/8 inches • Uffizi Gallery, Florence

Plate 93

Jacquemart de HESDIN
Madonna and Child, 1375–1400 A.D.
silverpoint on boxwood
5⅛ x 2¾ inches
Pierpont Morgan Library, New York

Bibliography

Benesch, O. "Die Zeichnung," *Europäische Kunst um 1400* (Europarat Exhibition), Vienna, 1962, pp. 240 ff.

Bostico, Sergio, and Garbini, Giovanni. "Drawing in Antiquity and the Middle Ages," *Encyclopedia of World Art,* IV, 468-69.

Breuil, Abbe H. *Four Hundred Centuries of Cave Art.* Montignac (Dordogne), n.d.

Brunner-Traut, Emma. *Die Altägyptischen Scherbenbilder (Bildostraka) der deutschen Museen und Sammlungen.* Wiesbaden, 1956.

Degenhart, Bernhard. "Autonome Zeichnungen bei mittelalterlichen Künstlern," *Münchner Jahrbuch der bildenden Kunst,* 3 Folge, Band 1, 1950, pp. 93-158.

Grotanelli, Vinigi L. "Drawing in Primitive Cultures," *Encyclopedia of World Art,* IV, 462-68.

Hahnloser, Hans R. *Villard de Honnecourt.* Vienna, 1935.

Henry, Francoise. *Irish Art in the Early Christian Period.* London, 1940.

Illustrated and Calligraphic Manuscripts, Harvard College Library. Cambridge (Massachusetts), 1955.

Maringer, Johannes, and Bandi, Hans-Georg. *Art in the Ice Age.* New York, 1953.

Oakeshott, W. *The Artists of the Winchester Bible.* 1945.

Oertel, R. "Wandmalerei und Zeichnung in Italien," *Mitteilungen des Kunsthist. Inst. Florenz,* 5, 1940.

Parrot, André. *Babylon and Nineveh.* New York, 1963.

Parrot, André. *Sumer.* New York, 1961.

Pfuhl, Ernst. *Masterpieces of Greek Drawing and Painting.* New York, 1926.

Robertson, Martin. *Greek Painting.* Geneva, 1959.

Rumpf, Andreas. "Greece and Rome [Drawing]," *Encyclopedia of World Art,* IV, 469-74.

Salvini, Roberto. "Medieval Europe [Drawing]," *Encyclopedia of World Art,* IV, 474-78.

Scheller, R. W. *A Survey of Medieval Model Books.* Haarlem, 1963.

Smith, W. Stevenson. *Art and Architecture of Ancient Egypt.* Hammondsworth (Middlesex), 1958.

Swarzenski, Hanns. *Monuments of Romanesque Art.* Chicago, 1953.

Swindler, Mary H. *Ancient Painting.* New Haven, 1929.

de Tolnay, Charles. *History and Technique of Old Master Drawings.* New York, 1943.

Vaudier d'Abbadie, J. *Catalogue des ostraca figurés de Deir-el-Medineh.* Cairo, 1936.

Weitzmann, Kurt. *Ancient Book Illustration.* Cambridge (Massachusetts), 1959.

Weitzmann, Kurt. *Illustrations in Roll and Codex.* Princeton, 1947.

Wormald, Francis. *English Drawings of the Tenth and Eleventh Centuries.* London, 1952.